U.S. Tax Payer's Reference Manual

Jimmy R. Friske

DISCLAIMER:

This information is presented for educational and informational purposes only.

Always seek the advice of qualified professional like tax advisor or attorney with any questions you may have. Never disregard professional advice because of something you have read.

Table Of Contents

Introduction

The following articles are a compiled report about the different elements of the US tax system, and the many facets of deductions, credits, qualifying dependents, the corporate entities, the sole proprietorships, and the everyday average citizen. There are many interesting facts and figures that are available to every American, absolutely free, through the IRS website, the problem however, is that much of the information that is available is in a language that seems foreign to readers looking for everyday, average wording. These articles, hopefully take much of the pertinent individual taxpayer information, and some corporate information, and put them into an interesting and entertaining format. Hopefully, as you read these series of articles on the US tax system, you will find that there are beneficial pieces of information here, and that you've not only enjoyed the reading, you've helped lower your bottom line!

401(k)

The 401(k) is a retirement plan implemented and provided to employees by their employer as a means to save for their retirement. Not only do many employers contribute to the employees 401(k) along with employee contributions (this is known as matching), but the contributions are pre-tax contributions; in other words the deduction is taken prior to calculating the state and federal taxes due on the wages. This helps not only the employee, but also the employer.

There are several variations of the 401(k) and depending upon your employer's status as a small business, and their ability to fund a 401(k), you may operate under a SIMPLE 401(k), a traditional 401(k), or The Safe Harbor 401(k). All the plans vary as to their contribution limits, the employers required matching contributions, and the level of administration and IRS reporting that must be factored into the plan upkeep. Let's take a look at each of the plans, and discuss some of the advantages and disadvantages of each.

The SIMPLE 401(k) is best suited for small businesses that have a reliable earnings stream. In other words, their cash flow and earnings level are fairly steady and reliable, and they want to establish an easily controlled method for providing for retirement funding. Quite often, many of the family members will participate in the 401(k) as a way to fund their own retirement, and offset some of the taxable income from the family business. The disadvantage in operating this type of retirement account lies in the fact that contributions made on behalf of the employee by the employer are not optional, and some form of contribution must be made each year.

The traditional 401(k) is the most often avoided plan by small to medium sized businesses, simply because of the massive reporting requirements, and the compliance testing that must be done each year. The administrative costs for the traditional 401(k) for a company of about 10 employees costs around $2000 per year to administer, and that doesn't include the setup costs or the costs of loan features. In addition to the optional features costs, there is the cost of offering many investment choices. Most of the 401(k) plans for small businesses that were surveyed had a much better rate of participation as well as lowered plan costs when only a few options were offered, instead of 10 or more.

The compliance testing that must be done with the traditional 401(k) are quite complex, and require much involvement by the accounting or payroll department of the business. Today, many small businesses outsource their payroll function, and include the 401(k) plan administration as one of the outsourced functions also. The greatest advantage to the small business is that the business is not required to contribute to the plan, unless there is a significant imbalance in the contributions of the highly compensated employees versus the lesser paid employees.

The Safe Harbor 401(k) is a spin-off of the traditional plan, except for the fact that there aren't all the compliance requirements and testing that must be completed each year. The Safe Harbor plan is best suited for the small business that has a steady revenue stream, and that is able to make a required contribution each year to the employee fund. The employer must make a 3% contribution to all employees who qualify for retirement funding, regardless of whether the employee makes a contribution; also, the employer contribution level for non-highly compensated employees must not differ more than 2% from the highly compensated employee contribution rate. In this manner, the employer is required to provide the same benefits for all employees, without all the compliance testing of the traditional plan. The Safe Harbor 401(k) is simple to set up, and can be accomplished within 30 days of the new year, and is simple to administer. The disadvantage to this plan is the required contribution rates, and if the business does not have a steady cash or revenue flow, it is not a recommended plan.

After examining the different plan options available for small to medium companies, there should be at least one that fits within any small businesses scope of operations. Providing retirement funding for small business family members, as well as all other employees is one of the greatest benefits a company can offer current and prospective employees.

Child Tax Credit

Now, here's a real savings to the individual taxpayer with children. The child tax credit is a direct tax credit that is available to provide credit to taxpayers with income below certain established levels. The maximum credit per child is $1000 and is first applied to reduce or eliminate the taxpayer's tax liability. How does this tax credit work, and does everyone qualify? Well, let's start with the last question first. Yes, everyone with children qualifies, however the tax credit phases out when income is above $110,000 for married filing jointly, $75,000 for single, head of household, or widow, and $55,000 for married filing separately.

Now, to answer the "how does it work" aspect; the best approach might be to simply break down the requirements, and explain each fully. The child tax credit is the responsibility of the Internal Revenue Service, and the credit issuance is determined through the tax returns the individual tax payer completes each year. Taxpayers must complete either the 1040 or the 1040A and the IRS from 8812. The IRS will then determine eligibility, and process accordingly; the requirements and limits change each year, so the individual's eligibility may change each year.

In order to qualify, a family must have earned at least $10,500 in income, and that figure will rise each year, according to inflation. There must also be at least one qualifying child; in order to be classified as a "qualifying child" the child must meet the following requirements: under age 17, claimed on your return as a dependent, must pass the relationship test (son, daughter, stepchild, grandchild, brother, sister, etc.), be a US citizen, and have a social security number.

During its original year of inception, many families with qualifying children were mailed an advance tax credit of either $300 or $400 dollars; but they were also told this would reduce their end-f-year tax credit, dollar for dollar.

The method used for determining the tax credit is fairly simple, and is not difficult to calculate; however, any individual taxpayer should seek the advice and assistance of a tax professional when preparing their tax return.

The credits, as stated earlier are claimed when you complete a 1040 or 1040A and file your returns with the IRS. Although many individual taxpayers pay for a professional to complete their returns each year, there are qualified preparers that are available free of charge each year, through the IRS; either way, make sure that you communicate your qualifications for the child tax credit, and check your return to see that the credit was applied.

The child tax credit, along with the Hope and Lifetime Learning credits are a direct means to affect the individual taxpayer's tax liability and offer some level of tax relief. This is meant to help parents with the costs associated in raising children, and educating them. Most often, the child tax credit is a way to alleviate the existing tax liability for middle-income taxpayers. For the extremely low income families, there is often no tax due, so there is no allowable credit. Although it does not help the poverty level families as a form of tax refund or tax-free income, it does help to alleviate any tax liability. The Earned Income Credit is used by many poverty level or low-income families as a supplement to their earned income.

Earned Income Credit

This is perhaps one of the best ways the government has introduced, to date, to raise families out of poverty, while requiring them to remain productive citizens. The Earned Income Credit is a refundable credit, that can be received even if no tax due—that makes it a negative income tax. It's the best investment in America's working poor to date, and it is becoming a widely used tool to aid the individual taxpayer.

The Earned Income Credit was brought to the forefront in 1998 by President Clinton, as a means of alleviating the taxing of working families into poverty. What has the earned income credit accomplished over the life of its existence? The earned income credit has provided some additional $3000 dollars per year to families of poverty level incomes; this has enabled better living conditions, better living standards, and a continued march to economic independence for many of these families.

How does the earned income credit work, and who qualifies, let's take a look. The earned income credit is a special tax benefit for working taxpayers with low or moderate incomes. For individuals earning less than certain specific levels with or without qualifying children, there is a tax credit that enables these individuals to receive a credit against taxes due, or a refund of income tax, that is known as a negative income tax. How do you qualify for the earned income credit? Well the qualification process is very simple; taxpayers with no qualifying children who earned less than $12120 over the year qualify for a small earned income credit. Taxpayers with qualifying children who earned less than $36,348 for the year will qualify for the earned income credit.

The maximum amount that can be refunded is $4400 for this tax year, and that is in addition to any refund of taxes already paid.   As you can see, the benefit here can be great at tax time, and many families rely upon this aid in order to get them through the year.

But, is it the great benefit it appears, or is it one more opportunity for abuse?   The answer here is yes, and yes.   The earned income credit is the great benefit that it appears, in that the only way to qualify is to have earned income.   This equates to the need and requirement to become a working citizen; you must work and make a contribution in order to qualify.   The opposite is also true; many individuals work only long enough to qualify, return to the welfare state, and then also receive a huge tax refund each year. The earned income tax credit should be amended to include a stipulation requiring the taxpayer to obtain gainful employment for at least 9 months each year.   This would eliminate the eligibility for welfare in most cases, and create the desired effect of productive, working citizenry.

In addition to the obvious opportunity for abuse discussed above, there's another abuse that is rampant among the poorer citizens of this country: individual taxpayers are claiming dependents that are really not theirs to claim. The refund however, is much larger is children are shared among eligible family members. Instead of only one individual receiving a refund for three children of at most $4400; you now can have two individuals receiving refunds of $2662 and $4400, respectively. See the problem?

Although there are due diligence tests that are performed by qualified tax professionals to determine a taxpayer's eligibility, there are some situations where even the best of preventive measures aren't enough. It is for reasons such as these, that we tolerate the minor abuses, in order to help the majority. It is a blessing and a curse at times to live in a country where we operate for the benefit of the majority. It means there are times we must simply turn a blind eye to minor abuses, in order to accommodate the major good.

IRAs

Today, more than ever individuals should be concerned about their retirement savings, and if they will have enough to see them through their golden years. Currently, social security benefits are all that many Americans have to see them through their retirement, and with inflation, escalating medical expense, and prescription drug costs, many senior citizens simply cannot make ends meet on their fixed incomes. In addition to these concerns, many of our citizens known as the "baby boomers" are reaching retirement age. With more and more of our population retiring, the need for adequate funding is an ever increasing concern for all individuals.

The Individual Retirement Account or IRA, is the original idea conceived to help the individual that had no retirement plan through work save for their retirement, tax free. The traditional IRA option allowed tax payers to invest in an IRA and deduct it from their adjusted gross income at the end of the year, thus saving them money on their tax liability. In other words, the savings was really a pre-tax deduction. Today, there are more versions available, and some have restrictions on the tax deduction you're allowed to take. Nonetheless, the savings benefit is still ever present.

With all the fluctuation of the stock market, investments that individuals had in the stock market, may or may not still provide adequate funding for their retirement. Many individuals that had retired and placed their funds in stocks have now found that they must return to work, even if only part-time, in order to maintain their current standard of living. That's a place no retired individual wants to be. The IRA plans offer less of a return, buy they're also a much safer option.

Contribution limits on IRAs have been increasing for the last several years, and currently for 2005 are at $4500 for non-working spouses, the same level applies. So for a household of taxpayer and non-working spouse, a combined contribution of $9000 may be made this year. In addition to the yearly contribution, for all individuals over the age of 50, catch-up contributions of $500 for each may be made. That raises the limit to $10,000 this year.

The only other concern the individual contributor should have is the tax deduction status of the contribution; depending upon your filing status, income level, and availability of a 401(k) plan at work, your deduction may or may not be limited. The masses will be able to take the contribution as at least a partial deduction; for the few tax payers earning more than $80,000 or $160,000 for spouses covered by an employee retirement plan, there is no deduction. However, for many of the individuals who would fall into this category, there are usually more options available than the simple IRA.

The taxes on the investment growth, and any dividends accumulated are deferred until the money is withdrawn, and it is then taxed as additional ordinary income when received. If for some reason you should need to withdraw the money prior to attainment of age 59½, you will be assessed a 10% penalty, with few exceptions; there are however a few of those "exceptions" that might apply to many individual tax payers. Withdrawals for the purchase of a first home, to pay for college expenses for yourself, your spouse or your dependents, disability, or payment of medical expenses that exceed more than 7.5% of your adjusted gross income and for substantially equal payments based upon your life expectancy are not assessed a 10% penalty. These are sometimes referred to as "hardship withdrawals".

As with any other type of investing, any individual that is interested in investing in an IRA, MSA, 401(k), or any other form of retirement planning, should seek the advice of a trained professional.

Medical Deductions

Thanks to the complexity of the United States tax codes, the system itself, and the variations of tax codes from state to state, completing your personal tax return and maximizing your deductions and exemptions to their fullest potential, is like trying to complete a mind-twisting maze. The average individual required to file a personal tax return has no grasp of the US tax system, and must therefore rely on one of the many tax professionals to complete their return. Quite often, deductions and exemptions are overlooked simply because of a lack of communication. The following article will discuss the medical deductions available to the individual tax payer, and the fact that qualifying for these deductions must be communicated to the tax preparer.

The medical deduction allowable on your personal federal income tax return is 7.5% of your adjusted gross income. The expenses you're allowed to deduct include medical, dental and eye care expense for anyone who qualifies as a dependent for your return.   If you are self-employed, the premium deductions you can take at a rate of 100%, and if it happens to be a better benefit, and you're self-employed, take the insurance premium deduction under your Schedule C deduction.

Who qualifies as your dependent, and what medical expenses incurred by that individual are deductible? Let's take a moment to clarify. A person will generally qualify as your dependent if they lived in your home for the entire year, you provided over half their support, and they meet the relationship test. And, oh yes, they must be a U.S. Citizen. What medical expenses are deductible?   I think an easier question might be what is not deductible?   You can't deduct expenses for which you are reimbursed, you can't deduct cosmetic surgery for which there is no valid medical reason for the procedure, and you can't deduct nonprescription medicine. That approach makes the list much smaller.

What information should you provide to your tax preparer? Information such as medical expenses you paid for yourself or your children the past year, any medical insurance premiums you may have paid; dental work, eye exams, laboratory expenses, overnight expense to travel for medical treatment and hearing exams to name the most common. Now I'm going to list a few things you might not have though about.

If you have trouble with your vision, and you require a Seeing Eye dog, the expense for the purchase and upkeep of the animal is a medical expense deduction. Your transportation expense to and from the doctor is deductible. Legal fees you incur in obtaining the necessary authority to treat someone for mental illness is a medical deduction. The use of artificial implants, such as teeth and limbs are deductible. Ambulance service is you're charged is a medical expense. Even having the lead paint removed from your home is a deductible medical expense, since many children are at risk for lead poisoning. There are some of the nontraditional treatment therapies available as medical deductions, acupuncture and Christian Science Practitioner fees are two of the more common, however, you should check with your service provider. Quite often, they will know if their services qualify as deductible.

As you can see, there are many items that are considered medically deductible that would not readily seem to be classified as a medical expense. There as also ways to maximize the items that are normally included in medical deductions, in order to get the most bang for your buck.

If you're receiving medical care that will be extended over the end of one tax year, and into the beginning of the next tax year, schedule as much of the expense during the last couple of months of the current tax year, that way you stand a better chance of including more of those dollars that are above the 7.5% mark of your adjusted gross income. If you are self-employed and must provide your family with health insurance, insure them as a part of your business; generally all members of the family will participate in a family business, therefore, you can enroll them as employees of the business and this makes the entire premium deductible.

Personal Deductions

Thanks to the complexity of the United States tax codes, the system itself, and the variations of tax codes from state to state, completing your personal tax return and maximizing your deductions and exemptions to their fullest potential, is like trying to complete a mind-twisting maze. The average individual required to file a personal tax return has no grasp of the US tax system, and must therefore rely on one of the many tax professionals to complete their return. Quite often, deductions and exemptions are overlooked simply because of a lack of communication. The following article will discuss the personal deductions available to the individual tax payer, and the fact that qualifying for these deductions must be communicated to the tax preparer.

The really big one that most all taxpayers are familiar with is the standard versus itemized deduction that removes a large amount of the tax liability. The standard deduction is $3200 per personal exemption claimed on the tax return. If you're a taxpayer and spouse, with three children your standard deduction would be $16,000. That's a lot of money to deduct from your tax liability. Again, however most everyone understands how this deduction works, and that the information to accurately configure this deduction is provided at the time of preparation and filing. What about the itemized deduction? Why are we given a choice of standard or itemized? We're given a choice because on the itemized deductions, or Schedule A of the 1040, certain expenses are allowed a deduction that might prove to be a bigger benefit for the taxpayer. What are these allowable deductions?

Medical expenses, certain taxes paid, mortgage interest expense, points paid on your mortgage, charitable gifts, casualty and theft losses, and unreimbursed employee expenses cover the vast majority. Sometimes, the taxpayer's expenses in a certain area for one year exceed what is considered the normal level, and filing itemized deductions creates a bigger savings than the standard deduction allowed. It is for this reason, that the taxpayer must be aware of these deductions, and make the tax preparer aware that an unusual situation exists. The stipulation that exists here is that often the deduction is limited to a percentage of the adjusted gross income.

What other deductions are available to take that directly affect the adjusted gross income? Some of these are not as well known, yet have a bigger impact on the amount of tax liability you will incur based on your individual tax return. Educator expenses or expenses you incur as a teacher in the education system are deductible to a certain level and are not restricted by the percentage rules of the itemized deductions. Health savings accounts, medical savings accounts, and individual retirement accounts are other deductions that are applied on a dollar for dollar basis. If you happen to be among the nations self-employed, there are additional deductions for an SEP, or self-employed pension fund, health insurance premiums expense, and one-half of your self-employment tax that remove tax liability, dollar for dollar spent.

Are you a student that pays student loan interest, or part of your qualified tuition and fees? Then you're also eligible for a dollar for dollar deduction. This has proven to be an exceptionally wonderful benefit for many of the non-traditional students returning to school in their thirties and forties, that struggle to pay tuition and fees. This is also deductible if you paid these expenses for a dependent child to attend college. The only thing to make sure that you guard against is double deduction. Don't take the deduction if your child is taking the deduction on their tax return. Generally, however, if a parent is providing the support for their child to attend college, the child doesn't file a tax return at all; usually they're still being claimed as a dependent.

Did you have to move this year, in order to keep your job? Did you take a new job that required you to move? Moving expenses is also a tax deduction that is tremendously overlooked, and not taken as a deduction. Why? Generally, the deduction is taken because many of the individual taxpayers that would qualify for the deduction simply aren't aware that the deduction exists.

As you ready yourself for the "blow" of the tax man's axe, keep in mind that we often can reduce the burden of our tax liability simply by educating ourselves about the basic information we should provide to our tax preparers. The better job we do in providing them with information, the better job they can do with providing us a refund!

Personal Exemptions

Thanks to the complexity of the United States tax codes, the system itself, and the variations of tax codes from state to state, completing your personal tax return and maximizing your deductions and exemptions to their fullest potential, is like trying to complete a mind-twisting maze. The average individual required to file a personal tax return has no grasp of the US tax system, and must therefore rely on one of the many tax professionals to complete their return. Quite often, deductions and exemptions are overlooked simply because of a lack of communication.

What are our allowable personal exemptions and how is the exemption rate calculated? The following article will discuss and define these terms, and what they mean to the average tax payer.

Personal exemptions for your tax reporting purposes refer to you, your spouse, and any dependents you may have in your household. The United States tax system makes an allowance for your family by allowing a deduction for each member, prior to assessing your tax liability. Although these rates have remained fairly steady over the past eighty something years, the level of income, and the tax levied on that income has shown an enormous growth rate.

The personal exemption for single persons in 1913 was $3000 and the exemption for married individuals in that same year was $4000. Not much has changed since 1913, in the way of personal exemptions.

The most interesting aspect in the area of personal exemptions, now that we've defined what they are and why we're allowed to take them, is that they have changed very little since the inception of income tax in 1913. When U.S. income tax was brought into existence, the average amount of income that was taxable after exemptions was 1%; for many Americans, their income wasn't even enough for them to file a tax return. Compare that rate with the current liability rate, and at least 10% of our income is taxable. That's a tremendous increase in revenue for the government, and a huge tax liability for the individual taxpayer.

On the individual tax form, also known as the 1040, your personal exemption information will directly follow your filing status. At this point, you must list all persons for which an exemption can be claimed that reside as a part of your household. Upon completion of the income section of the 1040, and the adjustments to income directly following, you will then be asked to compute an exemption rate, the number of persons claimed in the exemption section of the return, by a certain dollar value. This rate has remained fairly steady at somewhere around $3000 for each person claimed as an exemption. What effect does this have on your tax liability?

Well, quite often, the adjusted gross income level less the exemptions and standard deduction will leave only about 10% of your income as taxable income. And, most every individual taxpayer with a job and a W-2 will have already had at least 10% of the income deducted and paid as Federal withholding tax each week. What does this mean at the end of the year? The taxpayer will generally be due a refund.

Although the personal exemption rates haven't changed much since their inception, the addition of dependents and the standard deduction have helped to offset the amount of income that we tax. To further accommodate the reduction in tax liability, the exclusion of IRAs, MSAs, and SEPs from our taxable income has worked to create an even lower taxable rate.

Personal exemptions were an original part of the U.S. Tax code, and have been a constant throughout the history of the tax system. There have been many changes to the taxable income we report, the areas of income that are taxable, and the income exclusions that aren't taxable; but the exemptions have remained. Perhaps as insulation for the average individual taxpayer, who would have no capital gains tax breaks, very few pre-tax savings deductions, and no tax credits for employment taxes. An overwhelming majority of Americans receive a paycheck each week, and a W-2 at the end of the year. Their personal exemptions and standard deductions are their only breaks in the tax liability assessments.

Personal Income Tax Returns

Personal income tax, as we know it today, was originally enacted by Congressional law during the ratification of the sixteenth Amendment in 1913. Although we have experienced many changes to the system since that point in time, the importance of the individual income tax to the Federal Government's revenue as remained a constant. Today, half of the government's revenue is generated from the assessment of personal income tax due, and mounts into the trillions of dollars each year.

Some of the more significant changes to our tax law are discussed below and might surprise today's taxpayer, simply because our knowledge of the tax system is far removed from some of the earliest requirements, inclusions, and exclusions.

For instance, federal government employees were taxed on their income, but state and local government employees were exempted. Also exempt from the income tax levy was interest income from government bonds, federal, state and local. The exemption for single persons was $3000, and for married individuals it was $4000. Not much has changed, even though inflation has created major changes in our income levels, the exemption rates haven't changed in direct correlation.

Another important concept that has experienced much change over the years is the use of "personal income" in some tax liability instances, versus the use of adjusted gross income in some other instances. There are great differences in these figures, if you make use of the many deductions and exemptions that are currently a part of the individual income tax form, the 1040. Now, here's another important difference: during the tax systems inception, there was only one form used by all taxpayers, even business owners. Today, there are 3 different forms just for the individual tax payer's filing status. If you're a business owner, or if you own investment property, there are also many additional schedules for which you must separate your income away from the basic 1040 wages, salaries, and tips. This has been in an effort to encourage the small business ownership in American to expand.

Capital gains, of course have always received preferential treatment, but for many years they weren't taxed at all. It would seem the unfair exclusion of the wealthy individuals ability to invest and realize a profit, was in existence even then.

Many of the concepts we take for granted with our tax system today, weren't introduced all that many years ago. Tax tables, medical expense deductions, standard deductions, the definition of taxable income were established until the 1940s; earned income credit, alternative minimum tax, mortgage interest, and investment interest tax weren't addressed until the 1970s; unemployment compensation and social security benefits weren't taxed until the 1980s, and state sales tax and personal interest were excluded as deductions during the late 080s.

As you can see the United States tax system, along with the personal income tax return are fairly young institutions, and at times, still seem to be undergoing many changes, often at a pace much faster than the individual taxpayer can accommodate. The changes that often occur, to benefit a taxpayer aren't even general knowledge until it is too late to take advantage of the opportunity.

It's through the use of a professional tax preparer and excellent communication that an individual tax payer will see the greatest benefit of the tax codes and regulations. hanks to the complexity of the United States tax codes, the system itself, and the variations of tax codes from state to state, completing your personal tax return and maximizing your deductions, exemptions, and credits to their fullest potential, is like trying to complete a mind-twisting maze. The average individual required to file a personal tax return has no grasp of the US tax system, and must therefore rely on one of the many tax professionals to complete their return. Quite often, these deductions, exemptions, and credits are overlooked simply because of a lack of communication. available to the individual tax payer, in addition to the fact that qualifying for many of these benefits must be communicated to the tax preparer.

Schedule C Returns

Schedule C returns are used by sole proprietorships to report their record of earnings and expense in their business to the Internal Revenue Service. The complexity of the form, coupled with the interpretations of the tax code, often send small business owners in the direction of the CPA, or the tax professional in order to complete the necessary paperwork. But what information we will be required to provide to the tax professional preparing our Schedule C? Omission of vital information can mean the difference between a small tax liability, and a huge tax liability. Educating yourself about the information necessary to complete the form is the surest way to achieve the maximum benefit, and receive the minimum tax assessment possible. The following article takes a look at the information that you'll need to furnish, and where to find it.

The most important piece of information that you will be asked to furnish is your business income for the year. Depending upon your line of business, your receipts and records can be kept in a variety of ways. For some retail businesses, daily sales receipts may be all that is necessary; for others, invoices and service receipts may be the record that must be kept. Either way, the ability to provide your annual income will be the first item of business.

Next, your expense must be recorded. You need to remember here, that your tax professional will not require you to furnish all the receipts for the expenditures that you report; only the IRS will require written, valid receipts. However, in reporting the expenditures, you don't need to use dollar values that you cannot substantiate. Examples of expenses you incur in the course of business are your cost of goods sold, advertising expense, labor expense, insurance expense, office expense, licensing expense, and legal and professional services expense. While these are not all the examples of expenses incurred, they are the most common.

Your cost of goods sold is a computation based on inventory level at the beginning of the year, versus inventory levels at the end of the year; if you don't maintain an inventory, your cost of goods might only be actual monies spend over the course of the year in the production of your goods and services sold.

Advertising and all the other expense listed above are reported on Part II of Schedule C and are expenses incurred as a direct result of business operations. The sum of the expenses will be based on your actual expenditures; there are a couple of exceptions: depreciation and section 179 expenses. These two expenses are a little bit different, and as a result the records kept to track these expenses are a little different.

Depreciation expense refers the loss in value of a particular asset over the course of its useful life. The

Internal Revenue Service recognizes this depletion of value and allows for a deduction of the depletion, on a certain schedule. This value does not always coincide with the determined book value of the asset, and sometimes when assets are sold if there is a profit above the already depreciated value, tax will be assessed after the sale.

Section 179 deduction also relates to the depreciation of certain assets. Assets with a short life expectancy or assets that a business can use to offset net income can be depreciated all at once, for the year in which they are purchased, and up to a specified dollar value. The use of depreciation and Section 179 expense to offset taxable income is a common practice in business today. Usually, it can be used during the first few years of business to provide a cushion for the business, and to hold at bay income tax liability for a fledgling company.

Another form often associated with the Schedule C is the Expenses for Business Use of Your Home, or Form 8829. This deduction is allowed only if there is a net profit. Any expense for the business use of your home that is disallowed in one year because of a net business loss may be carried over to an upcoming year.

Well, that just about covers the Schedule C information.   As with any tax preparation, seek the advice and counsel of a tax professional.

Business Expense

If you've ever been in business, the crucial importance and the tax liability impact of the business expense you incur over the course of a year are tremendous.   In fact, many businesses only succeed for the first few years because of the massive impact of business expense on their bottom line.   This article will take a look at some of those expenses by category, and the necessary record-keeping that must be done.

The major categories of expense are utilities, insurance, interest, labor, and depreciation.   In operating your own business, there are certain necessary, an unavoidable, operating expenses; the utilities you pay each month are examples of those unavoidable expenses.   The most often incurred utility expenses would include water, electricity, waste removal, telephone, and cable expense. It would be impossible to operate a successful business, without access to the above listed utilities. These costs on a monthly basis will normally run into several hundred dollars, if not into the thousands of dollars; the ability to deduct these expenses, on the income tax return is a way to recoup some of the expense and avoid high tax liability.

Insurance expense can be a tremendously expensive business expense, but a necessary one. Not one lending institution will all money for a business to operate without being assured that there will be general liability insurance, renter's insurance, or Worker's Comp. insurance purchased by the business owner. Carrying insurance is just a continuation of the need for assurance that in the event a disaster should strike, the business will not be a complete loss. It should be noted here however that insurance expense can be an insurmountable roadblock if the business has not properly anticipated the expense associated with the purchase of the insurance; quite often, they insurance expense will depend in part upon the revenue generated by the business. Greater revenue you and profitability levels often increase the amount of insurance, you're required to purchase each year, and it also affects the premium that you pay each year.

Interest expense, is sometimes an optional expense; however, if you have a loan against your business you're going to pay interest expense. If you operate your business and purchase products own credit from a vendor and you don't pay the bill you will pay interest there, also. As with homeowner's mortgage interest, business credit interest is completely tax deductible to the business, but the business must be able to survive until the year's end in order to reap the benefit.

Labor expense will be the most money consuming expense, a business will ever incur. When you account for the wages paid, the taxes pay, and a liability associated we of the need to meet payroll expense on time. This can be listed as the single greatest contributor to business bankruptcy or failure. Of course, this is a two-sided coin. A business cannot stay open and operate without the necessary labor; the necessary labor will not stay and work without necessary pay. So if you are able to pay, your employee's wages, you will be able to retain employees. It should be noted here, however, that most often it's not the employee's paychecks that the business owner has trouble covering, if the tax liability that must be paid by the 15th day of each month. The tax liability has managed to accrue over the period of a month and often the business owner does not anticipate the enormity of the tax that will be due.

The last expense of business owner is able to deduct is known as depreciation. Depreciation is not a direct dollar paid expense for the business, it is however, and expense the benefits the business owner greatly during tax season. Any equipment fixtures or other capital investment, the owner has made in their business, will have what's known as a "useful life". The length of the useful life of the equipment will determine the amount to be depreciated each year. There are two different methods for depreciation, there's the straight-line method and there's the modified accelerated cost recovery system that used by most accountants for business owners to their benefit.

C Corporations

The C corporations are really the starting point for the use of a corporation as a form of business. The C

Corporation existed much earlier than the S, and is the chosen mode of organization and operation for all large businesses in America today. This article examines the formation, the regulations and the advantages or disadvantages to the corporation form of organization.

The definition of a corporation is an organized form of business in which the ownership of the business is held by stockholders, or shareholders-individuals who have purchased ownership shares in the business. The corporation is organized with a board of directors and officers. The board of directors is elected to make the business decisions that affect the overall business condition and financial health of the business. Officers are elected to oversee the day-to-day operations of the business.

The advantages of operating a business as a C Corporation are first, that your liability is limited, second, it is a perpetual legal entity, and third, the C Corporation can raise money by selling shares of stock to corporate investors. What does all this really mean? The limited liability aspect works in this manner: you are only liable to the extent of your investment. If you've only invested $5000 in a business, you are only liable for the value of the investment or $5000. The fact that a corporation is a legal entity and is perpetual means that even if one officer, board director, or shareholder should die, the business continues, often quite successfully. The ability to raise money is perhaps one of the best advantages. Many times, a business will need to increase cash flow, or fund the purchase of new equipment; if you can sell shares in the business, you have a built in way to fund those needs.

The most basic requirement for the formation of a corporation is simply the articles of incorporation, or the corporation charter. The articles of incorporation must be filed with the state government in which the corporation chooses to become an entity, and as soon as the corporation is formed, an organizational meeting is held to adopt the corporation bylaws; these are the rules established by the Board of Directors for the managing of the business. The responsibility for the overall management of the corporation is entrusted to the Board of Directors, who will then elect officers who are responsible for the day-to-day operations of the corporation.

One of the greatest advantages to operating your business as a C Corporation is concerned with the liability of the individual shareholders. When you purchase stock in a corporation, you are only liable to the extent of your investment; nothing further. This is a true fact, unless there is a situation where the corporate "veil" is pierced. Then the liability of the shareholders guilty of piercing the veil will be questioned. What does this term "piercing the corporate veil" mean? It means you do not keep your personal finances separate from the corporation's finances. It looks like the guilty shareholder is using the corporation in personal ways, and this increases the liability of the shareholder in question.

The great disadvantage is the "double taxation" of profits. Any profits shown by the corporation are taxed, and then any dividends paid to investors, are also taxed. The corporation receives no tax deduction for profits distributed to investors in the form of dividends, therefore there is a situation created for double taxation: the corporation is taxed on the profits, and when those profits are distributed to shareholders, they are taxed again. However, this is just a casualty of the situation: if you wish to have the business entity treated as a separate legal entity, it must also be treated as a separate taxable entity.

Corporate Income Tax

The current tax system imposed on corporations by the U.S. government is at best, a biased system; for corporations that have a net profit, taxes on those profits amount to a full one-third. So, if you're doing business as a standard "C" corporation, and you do manage to make a profit, you're going to owe Uncle Sam about 30%. That's an amazing figure, so let's look at some of the behind-the-scenes information that will help to enlighten us as to the "why" so much tax should be levied.

The first thing you must understand when dealing with the corporate tax structure, is that for the most part, many large corporations do not pay the complete 30% tax that would typically be levied against an individual if they were in the same situation; corporate accountants and the sheer process by which corporations must report their income, expenses, deductions, depreciation, dividends, and any other financial transactions allows for huge deductions that typically offset any tax due. This concept is a major topic of discussion today, as we attempt to better control and regulate corporate accountability for their finances.

When you have large corporations that are obviously reporting earnings and paying dividends, yet they pay no tax, you should be tipped off to the fact that there is a problem. How to fix that problem, may be another subject altogether.

The latest proposals have been to eliminate the corporate tax altogether. This would shift the tax burden to the individuals of this country; that is a tremendous shift from the post-war era of the Second World War, when corporations and individuals shared the responsibility almost equally. Thanks to the lobbying done by corporate lobbyists over the last thirty years, we've finally reached the point of no return. The latest proposals have come from within the halls of Congress to eliminate corporate tax, and let the average taxpayer assume all the responsibility.

In case some of you have noticed, we as individual citizens are losing more and more of our take home pay each year, to taxes of some kind. Medicare, social security, and income taxes take a larger portion of our dispensable income each year. This would take a step closer to making even more of our income the property of the tax man.

What about this seems unfair? As pointed out by the individuals who are in favor of eliminating corporate tax, it would encourage capital investment and job growth in this country and that is absolutely true, it theoretically would do just that. But since when does theory actually work in practice? Communism works in theory. Many individuals believe it is simply another way to provide tax-free income to CEOs, and Board Members. The latest scandals such as Enron and HealthSouth have shown this country real hard evidence of the corporate abuses that are rampant in this country, and so far uncontrolled. The Sarbanes-Oxley Act has taken great steps toward greater accountability on the part of the corporate environment, but elimination of corporate tax is simply a legal way to avoid paying the tax.

The most interesting information I have found in researching this topic, is the fact that the media has paid little or no attention to these issues, thus allowing the purported growth of the corporate lobbyists to go virtually unnoticed by the American public. While mush emphasis has been placed on the Social Security issues we face, nothing has been mentioned about the loss of revenue we've experienced over the last thirty to forty years because of the decreased taxation of corporate America.

Where have tax laws and law makers turned to accommodate the decrease in corporate tax? There have been increases in individual tax liability and there has been an increase in sales tax. The sales tax affects the poorer of this country as a percentage of income, than the rich. The loss of revenue from the corporate structure of this country have led to starved educational systems, cities and counties that are revenue poor, and a economic system for the poor that only becomes harder to sustain.

When you factor in the ability of the wealthy and the corporate entities of this country to hire brilliant accountants that find loopholes in the tax system, and relieve their clients entirely of their tax liability, you cannot believe that the current system operates for the people, by the people, can you?

Cost of Goods Sold

If you're in business you are already familiar with the words "cost of goods sold"; but, for the remaining readers, cost of goods sold refers to the materials needed to produce whatever it is you're selling. If you're in the service industry, your cost of goods sold is relatively small, since providing a service doesn't require you to purchase additional materials to produce the service. But, if you're actually making a product, you must purchase materials to manufacture a product in some way.

There is a distinct difference between the cost of goods sold and business expense items, and in this article we're going to concentrate on cost of goods items, and differentiating them from business expense items.

When you complete your Schedule C for sole proprietorships, or the S Corporation or C Corporation return known as 1120 or 1120S have an entire section devoted to cost of goods sold and determining that exact value. If your business maintains an inventory, it too will play a part in determining your cost of goods value; even contract labor will play a role in determining your cost of goods sold. Let's take a look now at the information that is normally included in your cost of goods sold.

To begin, you need your inventory levels at the beginning of the year; technically, this should agree with your ending inventory value from the year prior. It should simply be a carryover of the total from the previous year's return. If you use a computer to calculate your tax, it will automatically carryover.

The next piece of information you'll need is a record of your purchases for the preceding year. Your purchases will include any materials purchased direct consumption in the production of the materials you sell. Purchases in this section of the return have nothing to do with the indirect costs involved in preparing a product for sale, or in making the sale, such as the advertising or insurance that your purchase in order to operate a business or make buyers aware of your product for sale.

Next in line is your cost of labor. The cost of labor does not include your wages and salaries paid. It does however include any costs associated with acquiring that labor, (such as workman's compensation insurance, recruiting fees, etc.) even the use of contract labor in the production of the goods for sale is included in this area.

Additional 263A costs, unless you actually incur those kinds of costs, you won't even know what the form is asking for. Section 263A requires that the tax entity capitalize the direct and indirect costs that benefit or are incurred by reason in the production activity of the business. Businesses that would normally incur these types of expenses that come to mind automatically are film producers, video companies, drilling companies involved in some research and development of a large area, and some manufacturing facilities.

Other costs are any other costs that cannot be classified into any of the previous categories, but are directly related to the cost of producing goods for sale. Since we operate in such a diverse and complex business environment, many expenses may be considered just that, a business expense in one area, but are vital to the production of a product for another business, therefore, should be included in the cost of goods sold. This is the purpose of the "other" costs area.

Finally, you must perform an inventory at year's end; this determines how much of your materials purchased are left on hand, and weren't actually used for the current year's cost of goods sold. If left unchecked, many business owners could stockpile inventory in years when there might be a tax due, in order to offset the calculation of the tax liability. This figure will also be used on the next year's return as your inventory for the beginning of the year.

When you finish collecting this information, it's merely a process of adding and subtracting in order to determine exactly what figure is to be used for your cost of goods sold, and for what profit your business will attribute a tax liability.

Labor/Employment Taxes

If you have employees, then you are responsible for payroll taxes. The term payroll taxes lumps all the different forms of employment taxes into one category known as "payroll tax". In reality, payroll taxes encompass Federal and state income tax withholding, social security and Medicare taxes (also known as FICA), Federal unemployment tax (FUTA), and any state and local unemployment taxes assessed. Payroll taxes are deducted each pay period from an employees gross pay and the remaining money that is distributed to the employee is what is known as "net pay". In addition to any taxes deducted from an employee's wages, there is a social security and Medicare liability incurred by the employer. As an employer, you must match the social security and Medicare amounts withheld for each employee. This is what's known as the employer paid contribution. Until recently, most employers reported and paid payroll taxes quarterly; however, with the advent of the EFTPS, or Electronic Federal Tax Deposit System, taxes are now paid on a monthly basis by all employers. The payroll taxes may also be paid via a tax coupon that is taken to your bank and presented with the monies to cover the payroll taxes due; this must be filed by the 15th day of each month.

Every quarter, a Form 941 (or 943 for Agricultural employees) must be filed with the IRS and the amounts reported on the 941 should reconcile to the amounts turned in each month via the tax coupon or the EFTPS. At the end of the tax year, a Form 940 or information return must also be filed and all amounts reconciled and balanced between the Form 941, 940, and the W-2 forms and information returns filed.

If you are a small business with employees, or you plan to begin operating a business with employees, you need to understand your tax responsibilities as an employer; how can you accomplish this? The IRS provides links to all the relevant Forms and Publications via their internet site at www.IRS.gov; here you will find definitions and terms associated with employees from the onset of hiring, to termination. W-4's, W-2's, I-9's, all the employment taxes you will be responsible for reporting, and all the rates associated with those taxes will be listed on this website. The IRS also provides you with information concerning recordkeeping, employment eligibility verification, benefit and retirement plans, and even the definition to be used in order to determine if someone is an employee or an independent contractor, it's all there. There is a tremendous benefit to be had by investing the time and resources necessary to understand and comply with all the federal, state, and local regulations concerned with employees and payroll taxes; however, you should also frequently seek the advice of a qualified tax professional, your accountant.

Over the last several years, the limits and percentages for the deduction liabilities have been raised in order to ensure the continuation of the Social Security and Medicare programs as we know them today. The problem facing many employers and payroll professionals now is the maintenance of the system and the update of changes in percentage rates and income withholding rates.

Each year, you will be responsible for maintaining the withholding records on every employee, along with ensuring that the correct percentages are withheld, based on the current year's earning levels. For wages above the current limit of $87,000, there are no Medicare or social security taxes withheld; however, the federal and state income tax continues, there is no limit for this taxation.

In recent years, we have all heard the rage over the lack of proper funding for the Social Security and Medicare fund; what many of the mid-range wage earners in America understand, however, is that they're earnings are being taxed enough. How do we solve this apparently looming problem of funding? Well, the jury is still out on this one, but someone will have to make a decision soon, and I'm sure it will affect the vast majority of the millions of average wage earners, as they represent the biggest pot of money.

Medicare Tax

In 1965, Congress enacted the Social Security Act, and established the Medicare tax as a way to care for the elderly in this country. In addition to the creation of Medicare, Medicaid was also established, and both operated under the Social Security Administration's supervision; The SSA was a division of the Health, Education and Welfare Department. Since that point in time, many changes to the tax, the administration of the program, and the eligibility of the recipients have seen much change. This article discusses some of the basic information about this tax, and what that means to the average citizen.

In 2001, the Health Care Financing Administration, or the HCFA was renamed to the Centers for Medicare and Medicaid Services or CMS; this is the administration that currently oversees the Medicare program. Medicare, as it exists today, is the national health insurance program for people age 65 or older, some persons with disabilities, and people with permanent kidney failure requiring dialysis or a kidney transplant.

The tax deducted from employees or wage earners paychecks each week is the monies used to fund this health insurance program, and everyone who earns wages must pay a certain percentage to the Medicare tax program.

Who is responsible for this tax? The employee and the employer pay a share of the tax, and each is an equal contribution. Since the inception of the Medicare tax, the rates of contribution have continued to increase, and the minimum wage earner typically bears the majority of the contribution responsibility.

What are the benefits associated with Medicare eligibility, once you've paid your tax and qualify for participation? Actually, the benefits are amazing, and needed by the vast majority of older Americans. Since medicine has managed to prolong the average person's life span, and we are now living longer than ever, Medicare benefits are needed now, more than ever. Until the beginning of 2006, Medicare covered your medical, surgical, and preventive maintenance needs. Beginning with 2006, however, prescription medicine will also be added to the coverage provided by Medicare. The benefits are many, for the individual willing to learn about the options offered.

The current Medicare system is divided into three parts: Medicare hospital insurance, Medicare medical insurance, and now prescription drug coverage. The Medicare hospital insurance is known as Medicare Part A, the medical insurance coverage is Part B, and Prescription Drug Coverage is simply known as that. The tax that has been deducted from payroll taxes each week over the course of your working life, covers the Medicare Part A, or hospital insurance; Medicare Part B, is available for a monthly premium fee, and now Prescription Drug coverage is going to be made available for all participants, at an additional premium fee.

Medicare Part B has several options available, and with the advent of the prescription drug coverage option, more of these options are being reviewed and discussed among the elderly of this country. What are the options available, and what do they mean for participants? Medicare now allows for covered participants to be enrolled as a part of the Original Medicare Plan, or in what is known as Medicare Advantage Plans that offer HMOs, PPOs, Private Fee-for-Service plans and other Medicare Health Plans, that offer more options still. Which option is the best choice? The answer to that question will depend upon individual circumstances, and the medical needs of the individual.

The program as it exists today can be quite complicated, and many of our elderly citizens are struggling with the choices that are available, and how to pick and choose among programs they do not completely understand offered by a government that isn't offering a clear explanation of the choices available. While many of the services that Medicare is updating would actually benefit our older population, their choices in making information available to the older population and the confusion surrounding the programs has not been conducive to participation.

S Corporations

One of the most widely used, second only to the sole proprietorship, is the S corporation; what is the S corporation and how does it work? Let's attempt to answer those questions in the next few paragraphs.

The definition of a corporation is an organized form of business in which the ownership of the business is held by stockholders, or shareholders-individuals who have purchased ownership shares in the business.   The corporation is organized with a board of directors and officers. The board of directors is elected to make the business decisions that affect the overall business condition and financial health of the business. Officers are elected to oversee the day-to-day operations of the business.

The advantages of operating a business as an S Corporation are first, that your liability is limited, second, it is a perpetual legal entity, and third, the S corporation can raise money by selling shares of stock to corporate investors. What does all this really mean? The limited liability aspect works in this manner: you are only liable to the extent of your investment.   If you've only invested $5000 in a business, you are only liable for the value of the investment or $5000. The fact that a corporation is a legal entity and is perpetual means that even if one officer, board director, or shareholder should die, the business continues, often quite successfully.   The ability to raise money is perhaps one of the best advantages.   Many times, a business will need to increase cash flow, or fund the purchase of new equipment; if you can sell shares in the business, you have a built in way to fund those needs.

There are however certain qualification requirements for an S Corporation; they are as follows: the corporation must be a domestic corporation; the corporation must not be a member of an affiliated group of corporations; the shareholders of the corporation must meet certain requirements. Partnerships and nonqualifying trusts cannot be shareholders. Under certain circumstances, corporations can be shareholders; the corporation must have seventy-five or fewer shareholders; the corporation must have only one class of stock, although not all shareholders need to have the same voting rights, and no shareholder of the corporation may be a nonresident alien. Although these may seem like difficult requirements to meet, they really are not. Most of them are taken for granted by many business owners in their attempt to form a corporation, so commonplace are the requirements. The only requirement that is today posing a problem is the requirement that all shareholders be citizens, not nonresident aliens. This interprets into a problem if say, a European investor wants to buy stock in an S corporation, and it currently is not permitted. However, as we operate on a more global basis, we may see a change in this requirement.

The disadvantages to the S corporation lie in the restriction on the number of shareholders and the fact that the corporation must not be a member of an affiliated group of corporations. Sometimes, the S corporation grows to the point that more than seventy-five shareholders is a feasible reality, and the corporation could be bought as a subsidiary, except that this changes the S Corporation status; it must now re-organize its legal entity status.

In forming a corporation, there are some legal requirements that must be met, before a corporation is legally recognized in the state it has chosen as it's state of incorporation; a name must be reserved and approved, articles of incorporation must be filed with county and state officials, and board members, officers, and stockholder shares must be completed. Once the corporation is organized, then the Board of Directors will put together the Bylaws that will govern many of the actions that the Board may execute, and what is expected from the officers, and the day-to-day operations of the business.

Self-Employment Tax

Who must may self-employment tax and why? Well, if you're self-employed, you will be responsible for self-employment tax. How do you determine your liability? For the purpose of determining self-employment tax, you are self-employed if you are a sole proprietor, an independent contractor, a member of a partnership, or are otherwise in business for yourself. If you are a self-employed individual, you will have a Schedule C to attach to your Form 1040, and self-employment tax is computed on Form 1040, Schedule SE. Individuals must pay self-employment tax is they have net earnings of $400 or more and there are several sources of net earnings that are used when figuring your self-employment tax liability. In most cases, net earnings include net profit from a farm or nonfarm business; if you operate more than one business, your net earnings from self-employment are the combined net earnings from all your businesses. The upside to operating more than one business: If you have a loss in one business, it reduces the income from another. Self-employment tax is the self-employed individual's contribution to social security and Medicare taxes; the old-age taxes of employment. The only difference between the employee and the self-employed is the employee's social security and Medicare taxes are paid half by the employee and half by the employer, when an individual is self-employed; he/she is responsible for the entire amount.

There are alternative methods that can be used for figuring liability of self-employment tax and they are: The Farm Optional Method and the NonFarm Optional Method. These methods may qualify an individual to claim a larger Earned Income Credit or Child Tax Credit; they may also, however, increase your self-employment tax liability.

The maximum amount of earnings subject to self-employment tax is currently $87,000.00. Now, when figuring your adjusted gross income on Form 1040, you may deduct up to one-half of your self-employment tax liability and if you are member of the ministry or clergy you may request an exemption from self-employment tax from the IRS.

When must self-employment taxes be paid? Generally, the self-employment taxes aren't due until the end of the year, when your personal tax return is filed. Why is it this way? The self-employment tax isn't due until the end of the year simply because of the fact that many self-employed business owners don't file the net profit or net loss figures on their self-employment earnings, until the year's end. If there is a net loss, the self-employed individual receives a credit of self-employment tax due, in the amount of one-half of the amount due.

The self-employment tax is the self-employed individual's equivalent to the social security and Medicare tax deducted from employee's paycheck each week. The wage earner's taxes are configured by their employer and are deducted on a weekly basis. The self-employed individual isn't required to make weekly payments of self-employment tax, but they are held liable for the full 15.3 rate, that is split between the employee and the employer in wage earning situations. In general, however, if you expect to owe taxes in excess of $1000 for the year, you are required to pay estimated taxes each quarter.

In summary, if you are self-employed, have net earnings of $400 or more, and file a tax return, you will be subject to self-employment tax. To learn more about individual liabilities, exemptions, and alternative tax methods, please visit the online site for IRS Forms and Publications at www.IRS.gov . Topic 554,

Publication 517 and 533 will provide more detailed and situation specific information.

Social Security Tax

Every week that you work, there are taxes deducted from your gross payroll that are distributed to the Social Security Administration, along with other programs administered by the government. Of all the taxes we pay, social security is one of the most beneficial, one of the most watched. Why do we pay social security tax, and what does it potentially mean for all Americans? The following article discusses the social security tax regulations and what we benefit from the mandated deduction.

Social security tax is deducted from our payroll each week in order to cover a portion of our retirement income when we reach age 65, but also a survivor benefit, should we become disabled during the course of our working life, or die as a result of work-in which case the surviving spouse and children would receive a monthly income supplement to help them with their daily expenses.

Each and every day, we are bombarded with statements that want to make us aware of the dire straits our social security system and the gloom and doom picture we face in just a few years. This article examines the information available about our social security system, and asks the questions about its fate and ours.

The social security tax we know and pay today has become a greater chunk of our income with the passing years. And, as if this is not enough, it is the poorest of this nation that pay the most, since there is a cap on the income levels that are subject to the social security tax. Currently, any income above $90,000 isn't subject to social security tax. This presents a problem for the nations poor and the federal government's level of social security tax received. As more and more of our population begin to age, there are fewer and fewer based employees to sustain the fueled growth and maintenance of the social security system. Add to this the fact that individuals with wage earnings beyond $90,000 are growing faster than the wage base for employees who remain below the $90,000 level, and you have the makings of a disaster. The latest predictions place the collision date somewhere around 2017. That's not an extremely distant future, and it certainly will be a problem for the 45-50 year old wage earner.

So what has been proposed to deal with this growing problem? There are currently several proposed solutions to the problem, and all of them, with just a few exceptions point to higher taxation of the wage earners income. It is interesting to note here, that when income tax and social security, Medicare, and the many other "beneficial" programs the government has implemented to aid the general public, we have lost in the area of disposable income. In 1913, when the income tax program was begun, less than 1% of the average individual's income was taxed. Today, we pay roughly 10% of our income in tax. That's a staggering rate of growth, when you consider that our income levels have also tremendously increased too. The following paragraphs briefly outline some of the more popular proposals for dealing with the projected shortfall, and the effect it should have on "Joe Citizen".

Increases in FICA taxes; of course, this is a hard sell in the current climate, but by the time we reach 2017, it might look like a better solution than any of the others.

Increases in normal retirement age (NRA) have already begun, and it looks like it is going to be an ongoing process. As our life expectancy increases, the ability of social security to accommodate greater payouts, and a reduction in the working population continues, extending the NRA on past the age of 70 is a real possibility.

Privatization of social security; although on the surface this looks like a promising solution, it would take a special kind of citizen to intelligently, objectively, and rationally invest their 4% allocation wisely, and truly reap the benefit that social security has previously provided.

Selling bonds or printing money. The US Treasury does have the option to intervene and raise the money to accommodate the excess demand, but you increase the probability of runaway inflation when you begin to pump excess money into the economy.

What is the ultimate solution for this problem? No one really knows, simply because no one can accurately predict long-range models. 20, 30, of even 40 years into the future, accurate predictions are extremely hard to come by.

Sole Proprietorship

There are several forms of organization for a business; the most common for small business is the sole proprietorship. In this article we're going to define the sole proprietorship, and look at the advantages of operating a business in this manner.

In the formation of a sole proprietorship, there is essentially no separation of the business from the owner. There is no legal separation of the business from the individual, and if you operate a sole proprietorship, you are personally responsible for the debts and liabilities of the business. Quite honestly, it's the method chosen by the majority of business owners for this reason: simplicity. There is no need for hiring a lawyer, there's no need for corporate paperwork and fees, and you can be in operation tomorrow, theoretically.

This is a continuation of the entrepreneurial spirit upon which most businesses are founded anyway. The definition of entrepreneur is one who initiates a new enterprise, assuming all the financial risks associated herewith, and undertakes to provide or control its management. The sole proprietorship form of operation is simply a continuation of that risk-taking spirit that inspires so many of us to take the leap into business ownership.

The income of the business is reported with the individual's tax return on the Schedule C, "Profit or Loss from Business" and is attached and made a part of the personal tax return. Although the business information is reported on a separate schedule, all the profit or loss flows through to be reflected on the individuals 1040 or 1040A. This is one of the advantages to operating in this manner; the other advantages would be the freedom to make any decisions the owner deems necessary, without any further input, the flexibility that comes from individual ownership, and the tax benefit that comes if the business shows a loss; it directly affects the personal tax liability of the owner.

What are some of the disadvantages? The biggest would be the fact that the owner is the business, and as such is solely responsible for debts, damages, liability, and operation. This is known as unlimited liability. Other disadvantages are the owner's difficulty in raising capital, and the continuation of the business; if the current owner dies, then a new sole proprietorship is formed, even if it is inherited by a relative. As you can see, sometimes the disadvantages, once the business has reached a certain size, might outweigh the advantages.

Is the sole proprietorship the best way to operate? In some instances, yes. In others, the answer would be no. However, there are several other options of organization formation, such as the S Corporation, the C Corporation, the Partnership or the Limited Liability Corporation; the catch here, is that all these forms of business require the owner or owners to form a legal basis for the business, and generally all members will want to actively participate.

One of the great current incentives to operate a business as a sole proprietorship today, and one in which there is growing interest is the ability to establish certain tax exempt retirement accounts, such as the SEP, or a Self Employed Pension plan. Retirement accounts like these, allow the small business owner to put away a large sum of money tax free, that might be otherwise be treated as taxable profit income. This has been a problematic situation for many of the nations self-employed: how to safe for retirement, without having insurmountable taxes levied on those savings. Well, today thanks to the creativity of our law makers, and many business owners, the sole proprietorship has several retirement options, that the owner can make tax-free contributions each year to save for their retirement.

Now that we've examined many of the advantages and disadvantages of the sole proprietorship, and we've looked at the tax and personal liability issues, we can close with one final thought: the spirit with which many begin their business endeavors cannot be organized into one form of operation, it simply chooses to seize the moment. This is what continues to ensure the success of the small business, in any form.

1099s

What is a 1099 and who gets one? Well, here of late, this term is used more and more frequently as many employers are opting to use contract labor versus hiring employees, who can turn out to be quite expensive when you factor in the insurance, payroll taxes, and other possible liability. This article will take a look at the 1099, its purpose, who can receive one, and why.

The 1099 forms, if you are the recipient, should be furnished to you by January 31, 2006, and must be furnished and filed by the company furnishing the form no later than February 28, 2006. But which 1099 form will you receive?

If you are classified as an independent contractor, or you receive income that is classified as non-employee income, or miscellaneous income you will receive what is known as a 1099-Misc.; these are the information returns most often received for contract for-hire work, leased workers, or general contractor payments for which there is not a direct sale as a merchant to a consumer.

The other most often used 1099 form would come as a 1099-Int; this is a 1099 received for interest income purposes; whether the income be from a lending institution, or from the sale of a seller financed mortgage, the recipient of any income from interest will receive a 1099-Int. A close relative of the 1009-Int is the 1099-OID. This is an information return provided when you receive an original issue discount, usually from transactions related to mortgages served by the Federal Housing Authority.

Another 1099 can come as a 1099-B for barter exchange transactions. What does this mean? It means that instead of monetary payment, you received a bartered form of payment, an exchange of something other than money, with value attached in order to pay for a service.

Other less used 1099's are 1099-A, 1099-C, 1099-CAP, 1099-LTC, 1099-Q, 1099-R, and 1099-SA; the R, Q and SA are for retirement and social security payments, and are received by many retired individuals. The payments from IRAs, MSAs, Coverdell ESAs, and HSAs are reported on these 1099s. The 1099-A is received is there has been an acquisition of secured property, or an abandonment of secured property.

1099-C is received if there is a cancellation of debt, as from a bankruptcy proceeding, credit card default, or other failure of a maker to make good on a debt that the lender or seller can use as a tax deduction. The 1099-CAP is a 1099 used to report significant changes in corporate control and capital structure. What does this mean in laymen's terms? If you and several other individuals are in business together, as an incorporated entity, and 3 of you buyout another individual, you will be required to furnish that individual with a 1099CAP so that the individual reports any income or gain from the capital sale of stock.

A 1099 that we've not seen very much until recently, but one that I'm sure we'll see much more of in the not too distant future is the 1099-LTC. Long-term care and accelerated death benefits are filed on this 1099; with a larger segment of our population aging, this segment also known as the "baby boomers" will make more use of long-term care insurance and payouts, and many of them will receive these types of 1099s.

Although these are most often forms of taxable income to the recipient, this is not always a steadfast rule. For many of the older citizens, for individuals receiving the returns as part of a discounted program through the government, and for certain other situations, these are only information returns that do not result in added tax liability. For the rest of us, however, a 1099 usually means we have increased tax liability.

Capital Gains Tax

The current tax system imposed on corporations by the U.S. government is at best, a biased system; for corporations that have a net profit, taxes on those profits amount to a full one-third. So, if you're doing business as a standard "C" corporation, and you do manage to make a profit, you're going to owe Uncle Sam about 30%. Now, you add to that tax a capital gains tax that is levied on the investment capital of that corporation, and you have the makings for a tremendous tax liability, or do you? The actual income tax paid by corporations and the tax paid as a capital gains tax has diminished tremendously over the last thirty or forty years, and apparently not many of the citizenry of this country, nor the media are asking any questions. The general public doesn't ask because for the vast majority and understanding of corporate taxation is non-existent; why isn't the media asking? That's another issue altogether.

The first thing you must understand when dealing with the corporate tax structure, is that for the most part, many large corporations do not pay the complete 30% tax that would typically be levied against an individual if they were in the same situation; corporate accountants and the sheer process by which corporations must report their income, expenses, deductions, depreciation, dividends, and any other financial transactions allows for huge deductions that typically offset any tax due. This concept is a major topic of discussion today, as we attempt to better control and regulate corporate accountability for their finances.

As for the capital gains tax, it is at an all time low, and President Bush has given corporate America and even greater gift of capital gains exemption on foreign income. Could you imagine how excited the average citizen would be to find their income had been exempted for a couple of years from tax? Don't look for that to happen any time soon, as the average guy doesn't have expensive lobbyists in Washington working for them.

When you have large corporations that are obviously reporting earnings and paying dividends, yet they pay no tax, you should be tipped off to the fact that there is a problem. How to fix that problem, may be another subject altogether.

The latest proposals have been to eliminate the corporate tax altogether. This would leave only the capital gains tax, and would shift the tax burden to the individuals of this country; that is a tremendous shift from the post-war era of the Second World War, when corporations and individuals shared the responsibility almost equally. Thanks to the lobbying done by corporate lobbyists over the last thirty years, we've finally reached the point of no return. The latest proposals have come from within the halls of Congress to eliminate corporate tax, and let the average taxpayer assume all the responsibility. Of course, these are the same individuals who voted themselves a pay raise in the face of a huge national deficit and a sluggish economy.

In case some of you have noticed, we as individual citizens are losing more and more of our take home pay each year, to taxes of some kind. Medicare, social security, and income taxes take a larger portion of our dispensable income each year. This would take a step closer to making even more of our income the property of the tax man.

What about this seems unfair? As pointed out by the individuals who are in favor of eliminating corporate tax, it would encourage capital investment and job growth in this country and that is absolutely true, it theoretically would do just that. But since when does theory actually work in practice? Communism works in theory. Many individuals believe it is simply another way to provide tax-free income to CEOs, and Board Members. The latest scandals such as Enron and HealthSouth have shown this country real hard evidence of the corporate abuses that are rampant in this country, and so far uncontrolled. The Sarbanes-Oxley Act has taken great steps toward greater accountability on the part of the corporate environment, but elimination of corporate tax is simply a legal way to avoid paying the tax.

When you factor in the ability of the wealthy and the corporate entities of this country to hire brilliant accountants that find loopholes in the tax system, and relieve their clients entirely of their tax liability, you cannot believe that the current system operates for the people, by the people, can you?

Income Tax Refunds

Those are the words that every taxpayer would love to hear, yes, you're receiving an income tax refund. For many individual taxpayers those refunds can be obtained through Earned Income credit, a real refund of overpayment of tax, or through an overpayment from previous years. Once you determine you're receiving a refund, there are several options for actually putting that money in the taxpayer's hands. Standard paper filing, electronic filing with direct deposit, rapid refunds, and refund anticipation loans are the options we have the choice of exercising, and for many refund anticipating individuals, the rapid refund or the refund anticipation loan is the refund of choice.

Since the advent of the computer age, and the great invention of the internet, the Internal Revenue Service has been fairly quick to react to the benefit of electronic filing. The returns are filed much faster, refunds are made faster, and money due the IRS can be obtained faster. Let's take a minute to look at the different refund options, and what each offers the individual taxpayer.

The standard paper filing, although many are more familiar with this method of filing, is slowing reaching obsolescence. There will soon come a time that the old system of paper filing will be entirely eliminated and replaced by the electronic filing methods. If you are still one of the dying numbers of Americans who files a paper return, you should anticipate receiving a refund in about 6 weeks; today, thanks to the great use of the internet, 6 weeks to receive a refund, seems like an extremely long time.

The rapid refund, that is rapidly replacing the standard paper filing, is an electronic method used for filing your tax return, and allowing you to receive your refund in about 10-14 days. Much faster than the six weeks it used to take. There are usually no excess fees attached to this type of filing, and returns may be filed for free through many local, public access facilities.

The refund anticipation loan, however, is a little different. These must be administered by a tax professional through an established alliance with a financial and lending institution. There are several excellent choices available, and many qualified tax professionals to complete your tax return, you will however be required to pay a loan fee or a small interest fee for the opportunity to obtain an anticipation loan. There are several restrictions placed on receiving a refund anticipation loan, and some of the restrictions may affect many people.

For example, if you owe back taxes, back child support, or liens and judgments, you can't qualify for the refund anticipation loan. Most often, the individuals who apply for and use the refund anticipation loan are recipients of earned income credit, and their refunds are usually well into the thousands of dollars. The refund anticipation loan can be processed in as little as 3 hours, and back in the hand of the tax payer by late afternoon; this is provided everything works exactly as planned.   The higher interest rates charged by the bank product providers, and the higher processing fees charged by the tax preparers, equate to less money for the tax payer, but many of these individuals don't even blink when told how much it will be to process their return, they just want the refund immediately.   This is just one more example of the instant gratification upon which our society chooses to operate.

Even for individuals filing with the electronic returns, and choosing to have their funds direct deposited, the turn around time is usually no more than 10 to 15 days. You would think that a turn around of less than 2 weeks would be quick enough for many taxpayers, but typically, the bigger the refund, the faster the necessary return.

It would seem to me, that this is just another way for the system to profit from the poor; as it is usually the poor that qualify for the earned income credit refunds, and these can be extremely large, especially for families with 2 or 3 dependents.

Legal Entities and Tax Liabilities

The definition of a corporation is an organized form of business in which the ownership of the business is held by stockholders, or shareholders-individuals who have purchased ownership shares in the business. The corporation is organized with a board of directors and officers. The board of directors is elected to make the business decisions that affect the overall business condition and financial health of the business. Officers are elected to oversee the day-to-day operations of the business. The corporation exists as a legal entity in and of itself. Today, the latest proposal is to relieve this legal entity of its tax liability. Let's take a look at the different tax structures of the corporations, and how this proposal will affect our corporate community.

One of the greatest advantages to operating your business as a C Corporation is concerned with the liability of the individual shareholders. When you purchase stock in a corporation, you are only liable to the extent of your investment; nothing further. This is a true fact, unless there is a situation where the corporate "veil" is pierced. Then the liability of the shareholders guilty of piercing the veil will be questioned. What does this term "piercing the corporate veil" mean? It means you do not keep your personal finances separate from the corporation's finances. It looks like the guilty shareholder is using the corporation in personal ways, and this increases the liability of the shareholder in question.

The great disadvantage is the "double taxation" of profits. Any profits shown by the corporation are taxed, and then any dividends paid to investors, are also taxed. The corporation receives no tax deduction for profits distributed to investors in the form of dividends, therefore there is a situation created for double taxation: the corporation is taxed on the profits, and when those profits are distributed to shareholders, they are taxed again. However, this is just a casualty of the situation: if you wish to have the business entity treated as a separate legal entity, it must also be treated as a separate taxable entity.

The situation created by the formation and operation of an S Corporation differs from that of a C

Corporation, in that net profit and net losses are flowed through to the shareholders, via a K-1. Generally, S Corporations are formed by small businesses or family owned situations when there is a need for liability protection, but the business is not large enough to support the operating conditions of a C Corporation. This is a better tax situation for the small business owner, but does not relieve them entirely of tax liability.

However, the current tax system imposed on corporations by the U.S. government is at best, a biased system; for corporations that have a net profit, taxes on those profits amount to a full one-third. So, if you're doing business as a standard "C" corporation, and you do manage to make a profit, you're going to owe Uncle Sam about 30%. That's an amazing figure, so let's look at some of the behind-the-scenes information that will help to enlighten us as to the "why" so much tax should be levied.

The first thing you must understand when dealing with the corporate tax structure, is that for the most part, many large corporations do not pay the complete 30% tax that would typically be levied against an individual if they were in the same situation; corporate accountants and the sheer process by which corporations must report their income, expenses, deductions, depreciation, dividends, and any other financial transactions allows for huge deductions that typically offset any tax due. This concept is a major topic of discussion today, as we attempt to better control and regulate corporate accountability of their finances.

The latest proposals have been to eliminate the corporate tax altogether. This would shift the tax burden to the individuals of this country; that is a tremendous shift from the post-war era of the Second World War, when corporations and individuals shared the responsibility almost equally. Thanks to the lobbying done by corporate lobbyists over the last thirty years, we've finally reached the point of no return. The latest proposals have come from within the halls of Congress to eliminate corporate tax, and let the average taxpayer assume all the responsibility.

When you factor in the ability of the wealthy and the corporate entities of this country to hire brilliant accountants that find loopholes in the tax system, and relieve their clients entirely of their tax liability, you cannot believe that the current system operates for the people, by the people, can you?

Penalties on IRAs, MSAs, and 401(k) s

The 401(k) is a retirement plan implemented and provided to employees by their employer as a means to save for their retirement. Not only do many employers contribute to the employees 401(k) along with employee contributions (this is known as matching), but the contributions are pre-tax contributions; in other words the deduction is taken prior to calculating the state and federal taxes due on the wages. This helps not only the employee, but also the employer.

There are several variations of the 401(k) and depending upon your employer's status as a small business, and their ability to fund a 401(k), you may operate under a SIMPLE 401(k), a traditional 401(k), or The Safe Harbor 401(k). All the plans vary as to their contribution limits, the employers required matching contributions, and the level of administration and IRS reporting that must be factored into the plan upkeep. Let's take a look at each of the plans, and discuss some of the advantages and disadvantages of each.

The compliance testing that must be done with the traditional 401(k) are quite complex, and require much involvement by the accounting or payroll department of the business. Today, many small businesses outsource their payroll function, and include the 401(k) plan administration as one of the outsourced functions also. The greatest advantage to the small business is that the business is not required to contribute to the plan, unless there is a significant imbalance in the contributions of the highly compensated employees versus the lesser paid employees.

The Safe Harbor 401(k) is a spin-off of the traditional plan, except for the fact that there aren't all the compliance requirements and testing that must be completed each year. The Safe Harbor plan is best suited for the small business that has a steady revenue stream, and that is able to make a required contribution each year to the employee fund. The employer must make a 3% contribution to all employees who qualify for retirement funding, regardless of whether the employee makes a contribution; also, the employer contribution level for non-highly compensated employees must not differ more than 2% from the highly compensated employee contribution rate. In this manner, the employer is required to provide the same benefits for all employees, without all the compliance testing of the traditional plan. The Safe Harbor 401(k) is simple to set up, and can be accomplished within 30 days of the new year, and is simple to administer. The disadvantage to this plan is the required contribution rates, and if the business does not have a steady cash or revenue flow, it is not a recommended plan.

After examining the different plan options available for small to medium companies, there should be at least one that fits within any small businesses scope of operations. Providing retirement funding for small business family members, as well as all other employees is one of the greatest benefits a company can offer current and prospective employees.

The IRA, individual retirement account, and an MSA, or medical savings account, works along the same premise, only the contributions are made in lump sum amounts, generally, at the end or just prior to the end of the tax year. For some, the IRA contribution made be made as late as April 15 of the upcoming tax year and deducted in the previous year. The individual contributions are made not through a company plan, but simply by the individual as an alternative means of acquiring savings to be used for retirement.

The taxes on the investment growth, and any dividends accumulated are deferred until the money is withdrawn, and it is then taxed as additional ordinary income when received. If for some reason you should need to withdraw the money prior to attainment of age 59½, you will be assessed a 10% penalty, with few exceptions; there are however a few of those "exceptions" that might apply to many individual tax payers. Withdrawals for the purchase of a first home, to pay for college expenses for yourself, your spouse or your dependents, disability, or payment of medical expenses that exceed more than 7.5% of your adjusted gross income and for substantially equal payments based upon your life expectancy are not assessed a 10% penalty. These are sometimes referred to as "hardship withdrawals".

Rapid Refunds

Those are the words that every taxpayer would love to hear, yes, you're receiving an income tax refund. For many individual taxpayers those refunds can be obtained through Earned Income credit, a real refund of overpayment of tax, or through an overpayment from previous years. Once you determine you're receiving a refund, there are several options for actually putting that money in the taxpayer's hands. Standard paper filing, electronic filing with direct deposit, rapid refunds, and refund anticipation loans are the options we have the choice of exercising, and for many refund anticipating individuals, the rapid refund or the refund anticipation loan is the refund of choice.

Since the advent of the computer age, and the great invention of the internet, the Internal Revenue Service has been fairly quick to react to the benefit of electronic filing. The returns are filed much faster, refunds are made faster, and money due the IRS can be obtained faster. Let's take a minute to look at the different refund options, and what each offers the individual taxpayer.

The standard paper filing, although many are more familiar with this method of filing, is slowing reaching obsolescence. There will soon come a time that the old system of paper filing will be entirely eliminated and replaced by the electronic filing methods. If you are still one of the dying numbers of Americans who files a paper return, you should anticipate receiving a refund in about 6 weeks; today, thanks to the great use of the internet, 6 weeks to receive a refund, seems like an extremely long time.

The rapid refund, that is quickly replacing the standard paper filing, is an electronic method used for filing your tax return, and allowing you to receive your refund in about 10-14 days. Much faster than the six weeks it used to take. There are usually no excess fees attached to this type of filing, and returns may be filed for free through many local, public access facilities.

The refund anticipation loan, however, is a little different. These must be administered by a tax professional through an established alliance with a financial and lending institution. There are several excellent choices available, and many qualified tax professionals to complete your tax return, you will however be required to pay a loan fee or a small interest fee for the opportunity to obtain an anticipation loan. There are several restrictions placed on receiving a refund anticipation loan, and some of the restrictions may affect many people.

For example, if you owe back taxes, back child support, or liens and judgments, you can't qualify for the refund anticipation loan. Most often, the individuals who apply for and use the refund anticipation loan are recipients of earned income credit, and their refunds are usually well into the thousands of dollars. The refund anticipation loan can be processed in as little as 3 hours, and back in the hand of the tax payer by late afternoon; this is provided everything works exactly as planned. The higher interest rates charged by the bank product providers, and the higher processing fees charged by the tax preparers, equate to less money for the tax payer, but many of these individuals don't even blink when told how much it will be to process their return, they just want the refund immediately. This is just one more example of the instant gratification upon which our society chooses to operate.

Even for individuals filing with the electronic returns, and choosing to have their funds direct deposited, the turn around time is usually no more than 10 to 15 days. You would think that a turn around of less than 2 weeks would be quick enough for many taxpayers, but typically, the bigger the refund, the faster the necessary return.

It would seem to me, that this is just another way for the system to profit from the poor; as it is usually the poor that qualify for the earned income credit refunds, and these can be extremely large, especially for families with 2 or 3 dependents.

Refund Anticipation Loans

Those are the words that every taxpayer would love to hear, yes, you're receiving an income tax refund. For many individual taxpayers those refunds can be obtained through Earned Income credit, a real refund of overpayment of tax, or through an overpayment from previous years. Once you determine you're receiving a refund, there are several options for actually putting that money in the taxpayer's hands.

Although this sounds like the perfect end to a wonderful tax year, taxpayers are paying around $2 billion annually in order to receive a loan against their anticipated refund of tax in one day. The interest rates charged by many tax preparers and lending institutions can run as high as 2000 percent, and the taxpayers aren't even blinking an eye.

Since the advent of the computer age, and the great invention of the internet, the Internal Revenue Service has been fairly quick to react to the benefit of electronic filing. The returns are filed much faster, refunds are made faster, and money due the IRS can be obtained faster. Let's take a minute to examine the refund anticipation loan, and the advantages and disadvantages of using this method for filing.

For many taxpayers, and families trying to make ends meet on limited incomes, receiving those W-2s can be a very satisfying and thrilling time. Many of these families have struggled all year to make ends meet, borrowing money to sometimes fill in the emergency needs. Now, finally the opportunity to get back a lump sum distribution of needed refund money has arrived. Quick refund anticipation loans, and the tax preparers that offer them, have seemed like a dream come true to many individual tax payers. They tend to overlook the exorbitant fees, and the costs associated with these refund anticipation loans or RALs, and march right into the tax office, seeking their money.

Here's where the refund anticipation loan can become a problem: if for some reason, your anticipated refund should not arrive as anticipated, and then you, the taxpayer are responsible for repaying the tax preparer, or their lending institution. What if you are once again without any excess money? This can be a problem. For example, if you owe back taxes, back child support, or liens and judgments, you can't qualify for the refund anticipation loan

Many individual companies, such as check cashing services, payday loan companies, and even rent-to-own centers are partnering with tax professionals to offer the service either in-store, or the opportunity to make it a part of a purchase proposition. The individual companies that are partnering with tax preparers are hoping to gain sales dollars by having the taxpayer in house when they receive their money.

For individuals who choose to go to some of the more established professional tax preparers such as H & R Block or Jackson Hewitt, they will pay even higher fees to get the return filed and receive a refund anticipation loan. The national average was around $250 for the 2004 tax year, and may reach new heights this year.

The sad fact is, that many of the taxpayers who seek professional tax preparers to complete their tax return, could use the VITA service, or Volunteer Income Tax Assistance Centers and receive an electronically filed return for free. The refund is back within two weeks, sooner if you have a checking or savings account, and it doesn't cost the taxpayer anything.

The rapid refund, that is rapidly replacing the standard paper filing, is an electronic method used for filing your tax return, and allowing you to receive your refund in about 10-14 days. Much faster than the six weeks it used to take. There are usually no excess fees attached to this type of filing, and returns may be filed for free through many local, public access facilities.

Most often, the individuals who apply for and use the refund anticipation loan are recipients of earned income credit, and their refunds are usually well into the thousands of dollars. The refund anticipation loan can be processed in as little as 3 hours, and back in the hand of the tax payer by late afternoon; this is provided everything works exactly as planned. The higher interest rates charged by the bank product providers, and the higher processing fees charged by the tax preparers, equate to less money for the tax payer, but many of these individuals don't even blink when told how much it will be to process their return, they just want the refund immediately. This is just one more example of the instant gratification upon which our society chooses to operate.

Self Employment Pensions

As a member of the rank and file of self-employed, I can tell you that it is one of the most wonderful ways to make a living. It is also one of the best ways to never plan for retirement, and turn around at age 65, with nothing but Social Security to fund your retirement years. But, it doesn't have to be that way. Thanks to the creation and passage of the Self Employment Pension options, more Americans have the opportunity to save money, tax free, in order to fund their retirement years.

An SEP, or self-employed pension plan, is a simple way for the self-employed individual to setup a written plan for making contributions toward their own retirement. Yes, any other eligible employees must be covered also, but the plan is by far the simplest and least complex option available.

What are the basic guidelines for establishing a self-employed pension plan? You must execute a formal written agreement to provide benefits for all eligible employees and yourself. You must provide written information to all employees that will explain the SEP, and there must be an SEP-IRA setup for each employee. It's not even necessary to file the forms with the IRS, if you use what's known as a 5305-SEP; you don't have to obtain IRS approval or a determination letter.

You can set the plan up with a bank, insurance companies or other qualified financial institution. You then send the SEP contributions to the financial institution where the SEP is maintained. Is there any limit to the contribution amount or time of the contribution? Yes, and yes.

You must follow certain guidelines when establishing contribution levels so that your individual contribution does not exceed a reasonable comparative level for the employees. The contributions must follow a written allocation formula, and must not discriminate in favor of any one sector of employees, especially the highly compensated employees. Contributions do not have to be made each year, but they must follow the prescribed guidelines above when they are made. The limits set on the contributions you can make cannot exceed 25% of the employee's compensation or $41,000. The compensation does not include the SEP contribution.

There are other restrictions that can be placed on the contributions, but they are really too detailed to cover in an article of this nature. Let me just say that if you are considering a self-employed pension plan, seek the advice of a financial advisor, and follow the requirements exactly, as you and the employee may be penalized for contributions that exceed the income deferment limits.

If you exceed the contribution limits for one particular year, you can carry those contributions over with what is known as excess carryover contributions. The only concern you may have, is that once carried over, they will reduce the upcoming year's contributions, too. Now, there's also the option to "carry back" contributions, but the carry back is only an option for the preceding year. You cannot go back and pick up ten years worth of missed opportunities, otherwise one would never run out of contribution options, and there would tend to be a massive abuse of the retirement system.

Many business owners simply do not understand the retirement process, and for many years it was a very expensive proposition to fund retirement accounts, such as 401(k) s; the complexity was difficult, the expense large, and the small business owner simply did not have the available resources to offer a program like this. Today, the process has been extremely simplified, and the cost has been reduced to almost nothing. You no longer even need the permission of the IRS, with some forms.

The SEP retirement opportunities available to self employed persons today are some of the most opportunistic ever available. It is an opportunity that every business person should take full advantage and make the most of, no matter how impossible that might seem. There is always room to save a little, and as we advance toward longer life spans, better medicine, and a Social Security program that will under current limits, be grossly under-funded when retirement is reached, we should take every opportunity possible to save for our retirement.

Social Security and Our Current Tax System

Every week that you work, there are taxes deducted from your gross payroll that are distributed to the Social Security Administration, along with other programs administered by the government. Of all the taxes we pay, social security is one of the most beneficial, one of the most watched. Why do we pay social security tax, and what does it potentially mean for all Americans? The following article discusses the social security tax regulations and what we benefit from the mandated deduction.

Social security tax is deducted from our payroll each week in order to cover a portion of our retirement income when we reach age 65, but also a survivor benefit, should we become disabled during the course of our working life, or die as a result of work-in which case the surviving spouse and children would receive a monthly income supplement to help them with their daily expenses.

Each and every day, we are bombarded with statements that want to make us aware of the dire straits our social security system and the gloom and doom picture we face in just a few years. This article examines the information available about our social security system, and asks the questions about its fate and ours.

The social security tax we know and pay today has become a greater chunk of our income with the passing years. And, as if this is not enough, it is the poorest of this nation that pay the most, since there is a cap on the income levels that are subject to the social security tax. Currently, any income above $90,000 isn't subject to social security tax. This presents a problem for the nations poor and the federal government's level of social security tax received. As more and more of our population begin to age, there are fewer and fewer based employees to sustain the fueled growth and maintenance of the social security system. Add to this the fact that individuals with wage earnings beyond $90,000 are growing faster than the wage base for employees who remain below the $90,000 level, and you have the makings of a disaster. The latest predictions place the collision date somewhere around 2017. That's not an extremely distant future, and it certainly will be a problem for the 45-50 year old wage earner.

So what has been proposed to deal with this growing problem? There are currently several proposed solutions to the problem, and all of them, with just a few exceptions point to higher taxation of the wage earners income. It is interesting to note here, that when income tax and social security, Medicare, and the many other "beneficial" programs the government has implemented to aid the general public, we have lost in the area of disposable income. In 1913, when the income tax program was begun, less than 1% of the average individual's income was taxed. Today, we pay roughly 10% of our income in tax. That's a staggering rate of growth, when you consider that our income levels have also tremendously increased too. The following paragraphs briefly outline some of the more popular proposals for dealing with the projected shortfall, and the effect it should have on "Joe Citizen".

Increases in FICA taxes; of course, this is a hard sell in the current climate, but by the time we reach 2017, it might look like a better solution than any of the others.

Increases in normal retirement age (NRA) have already begun, and it looks like it is going to be an ongoing process. As our life expectancy increases, the ability of social security to accommodate greater payouts, and a reduction in the working population continues, extending the NRA on past the age of 70 is a real possibility.

Privatization of social security; although on the surface this looks like a promising solution, it would take a special kind of citizen to intelligently, objectively, and rationally invest their 4% allocation wisely, and truly reap the benefit that social security has previously provided.

Selling bonds or printing money. The US Treasury does have the option to intervene and raise the money to accommodate the excess demand, but you increase the probability of runaway inflation when you begin to pump excess money into the economy.

What is the ultimate solution for this problem? No one really knows, simply because no one can accurately predict long-range models. 20, 30, of even 40 years into the future, accurate predictions are extremely hard to come by.

There has never been a more welcomed term in the adult taxpayer's life, than the invention of the W-2 and January 31st; let's take a moment to examine the W-2, and what it really means to the average taxpayer. What information is found on the W-2, how do we provide the information for the W-2 and who is responsible for providing the W-2?

There are 20 "boxes" of information found on the W-2, and all pertain to the varying forms of compensation you may have received as an employee. Boxes 1 thru 14 deal with employee compensation on a federal level; boxes 15-20 pertain to income and any state liability due.   Wages, tips, and compensation, federal tax withheld, social security wages, social security tax withheld, and the information for Medicare all relate to your federal tax liability.   Boxes 7 and 8 have to do with receiving tip income, and the amount of the income that is eligible for social security tax.

Boxes 9 and 10 are for earned income credit advance payments, and any form of dependent care benefits you may have received, that are taxable income.   Boxes 11 -14 are for retirement plan income deductions; pre-tax contributions such as to 401(k)s, SEPs, IRAs, MSAs, and HSAs, would fall into this category, and any contributions made that are pre-tax contributions would be shown here.

Boxes 15-20 are for reporting earned income as it applies to your individual state, or the state in which you worked. Quite often, taxpayers reside in one state, and work in another. If this is the case, when you complete your tax return for the year, you will file a return for the state in which you reside, and the state in which you worked, as a non-resident filer.

When you receive your W-2, you normally receive 4 copies; one for your federal tax return, one for a state return, one for an additional state that may or may not be needed, and one for you to keep for your records.

There are additional boxes shown on the W-2 that are alphabetically identified, as a thru f. These boxes contain information about the recipient and the company issuing the W-2. Your social security number, your address, and your employee number if you've been assigned one. These boxes are also for your employer information, their federal identification number, their address, and telephone number is usually also listed.

What items may be included in your wages, tips, and compensation? Believe it or not, it can include more than just your income from your weekly check. Any benefits received as bonuses, prizes, awards, and noncash payments may be included in your wage and income information. If you receive payments from taxable benefits of a section 125 cafeteria plan, (if you choose cash payment) will be shown as wage income. Employer paid contributions for qualified long-term care services to the extent that the contributions are flexible and controlled in part by the employee are taxable. Employer paid child care services are also included as income to the employee.

When it comes to deferred payments, pre-tax and after tax contributions to a 401(k), an IRA, a ROTH IRA, or an HAS, some of the benefits and contributions made by your employer may or may not be included as taxable income, and must be included as other compensation. Quite often, income included in this manner won't be subject to federal withholding, but will be subject to social security and Medicare taxes, so it there fore must be included for those taxes to be properly computed.

Currently, there is no cap on Medicare tax in relation to the level of income reported; with social security, the limit is the first $94,200 of earned income is taxable, anything above that amount, is not. It should also be noted here, that any advance EIC payments, or advance earned income payments should not be taxed with federal withholding, Medicare, or social security.

Education Credits

What are education credits, who is eligible, and why should we take them? Well, let's start with the first part of the question, and work our way to the end. Education credits are tax credits available for qualified education expenses paid by the taxpayer in the furthering of their education. Qualified education expenses are defined as an expense paid during the tax year for tuition and fees required by an eligible educational institution for student enrollment and attendance. It really doesn't matter how you pay these expenses, only that the expenses are valid. Now, let's give some examples of expenses that are not qualified so that you can determine those that are qualified, and how you account for these expenses. Room and board, medical expenses, student health fees, transportation, personal living expense, insurance, course-related books, supplies, equipment, or any non-academic activity or non-credit course are not qualified expenses. What does this leave? Basically: tuition.

If you take a deduction for education expenses in any other area of the personal tax return, you cannot use that expense when figuring a Hope or Lifetime Learning credit. If you received tax-free assistance, such as a Pell Grant or scholarship, you must deduct that amount from your qualified expenses; however, most scholarships and Pell grant monies are taxable, so you may be taxed, but you can also get the credit. If you make any prepayments of tuition, you can use the prepaid amounts on your current year's tax return, provided you have followed all other guidelines.

Now, there are two different credits: the Hope credit and the Lifetime Learning credit. What are their differences? Well, first you cannot take them jointly; you must choose one or the other. The Hope credit can only be taken during the first two years of college, as defined by the educational institution, and cannot exceed $1500. The Lifetime Learning Credit maximum for 2005 is $2000. It cannot be taken in conjunction with the Hope Credit, even if your expense exceeds the Hope limitations. If your expenses exceed the Hope limitation the first two years, simply include the excess on your Schedule A.

Your credits are also limited by your level of income, and your adjusted gross income totals. So, when figuring these credits, you need to consider your current student status, as Hope will expire after your 2nd year of higher education, and your income levels, and your expense levels. You can take any excess expense deductions under your itemized deduction expenses on Schedule A, when Hope or Lifetime Learning is at their maximums.

Who is eligible to take these credits? You are eligible as a taxpayer or eligible dependent of a taxpayer that was enrolled as a student in an eligible educational institution. If you can be claimed as someone's dependent, they will be able to claim the education credit, not the dependent. Generally, dependent students' expenses will be claimed by their parents or legal guardians. Now, here is an interesting note: if you are a student, and you cannot be claimed as someone's dependent, only you can take the education credit; even if you are not the individual paying the expense.

Why would you take the credit? I think a better question would be why would you not take the credit? In case you haven't noticed, it can be very expensive to attend higher education classes. For anyone seeking to further their education, receive a degree, and pursue their dream, any tax credit that can be taken, is a helping hand toward achievement of that dream. Today, without furthering your education, you're almost positively sentenced to a lifetime of minimum wage earnings, and struggling to make ends meet. A college education is the fastest route still, to a better life, better wages, and the achievement of the American Dream.

Hope and Lifetime Learning Credits

What are the Hope and Lifetime Learning education credits, who is eligible, and why should we take them? Well, let's start with the first part of the question, and work our way to the end. Education credits are tax credits available for qualified education expenses paid by the taxpayer in the furthering of their education. Qualified education expenses are defined as an expense paid during the tax year for tuition and fees required by an eligible educational institution for student enrollment and attendance. It really doesn't matter how you pay these expenses, only that the expenses are valid. Now, let's give some examples of expenses that are not qualified so that you can determine those that are qualified, and how you account for these expenses. Room and board, medical expenses, student health fees, transportation, personal living expense, insurance, course-related books, supplies, equipment, or any non-academic activity or non-credit course are not qualified expenses. What does this leave? Basically: tuition.

If you take a deduction for education expenses in any other area of the personal tax return, you cannot use that expense when figuring a Hope or Lifetime Learning credit. If you received tax-free assistance, such as a Pell Grant or scholarship, you must deduct that amount from your qualified expenses; however, most scholarships and Pell grant monies are taxable, so you may be taxed, but you can also get the credit. If you make any prepayments of tuition, you can use the prepaid amounts on your current year's tax return, provided you have followed all other guidelines.

Now, there are two different credits: the Hope credit and the Lifetime Learning credit. What are their differences? Well, first you cannot take them jointly; you must choose one or the other. The Hope credit can only be taken during the first two years of college, as defined by the educational institution, and cannot exceed $1500. The Lifetime Learning Credit maximum for 2005 is $2000. It cannot be taken in conjunction with the Hope Credit, even if your expense exceeds the Hope limitations. If your expenses exceed the Hope limitation the first two years, simply include the excess on your Schedule A.

Your credits are also limited by your level of income, and your adjusted gross income totals. So, when figuring these credits, you need to consider your current student status, as Hope will expire after your 2nd year of higher education, and your income levels, and your expense levels. You can take any excess expense deductions under your itemized deduction expenses on Schedule A, when Hope or Lifetime Learning is at their maximums.

Who is eligible to take these credits? You are eligible as a taxpayer or eligible dependent that was enrolled as a student in an eligible educational institution. If you can be claimed as someone's dependent, they will be able to claim the education credit, not the dependent. Generally, dependent students' expenses will be claimed by their parents or legal guardians. Now, here is an interesting note: if you are a student, and you cannot be claimed as someone's dependent, only you can take the education credit; even if you are not the individual paying the expense.

Why would you take the credit? I think a better question would be why would you not take the credit? In case you haven't noticed, it can be very expensive to attend higher education classes. For anyone seeking to further their education, receive a degree, and pursue their dream, any tax credit that can be taken, is a helping hand toward achievement of that dream. Today, without furthering your education, you're almost positively sentenced to a lifetime of minimum wage earnings, and struggling to make ends meet. A college education is the fastest route still, to a better life, better wages, and the achievement of the American Dream.

Income Tax Season

The tax season for most all individual tax payers falls during January, February, and March each year. It's the time of year that most citizens' look forward to receiving a refund or they dread because they know a balance due must be paid by April 15th. But do you know how all that came to be? Let's have a short lesson in the history of the income tax and tax season in the United States.

In the beginning, from 1791 to 1802 the US had no individual income tax system. The country and its government were supported by internal taxes on alcohol, transportation, sugar, tobacco, and slaves. But, thanks to the War or 1812, the first sales tax was implemented for purchases of gold, silver and silverware, jewelry, and watches. Then, in 1862, when the Civil War came along, the first formal system for individual taxes was implemented, and we've been taxed since. Additional sales, excise, and inheritance taxes were also made a part of our tax system, and thus the individual began to pay, and pay, and pay. But that's not the end of the story.

The income tax law of 1862 established the office of Commissioner of Internal Revenue. This office was given the power over all matters of taxation, and the right to enforce any laws and regulations. Not much has changed since the income tax law of 1862, as far as the powers given to the Internal Revenue Service. The income taxation of the individual citizen has changed, somewhat drastically, however. The income tax was repealed in 1872, revived in 1894 and 1895 then laid to the side.

It wasn't until the 16th Amendment to the Constitution made the income tax a permanent part of the constitution, and a permanent fixture in 1913 and the growth of the Internal Revenue Service really began to thrive. The 16th Amendment gave Congress the authority to tax the income of both individuals and corporations that resulted in a tremendous increase in revenue. During the following 5 years, annual internal revenue collections passed the billion dollar mark rising to several billion dollars by 1920. Thanks to the next series of Wars, employment increased, and so did tax collections, rising even further into the billions of dollars. Withholding taxes were introduced in 1943, and this increased the number of individual taxpayers to well over 50 million; at the same time, tax collections increased by to $43 billion in 1945.

Every president since the term of Ronald Reagan has in some way, shape, form or fashion signed into law tax cuts that have affected the individual taxpayer, as well as the corporate tax payer. Almost every tax cut ever introduced, for some brief period of time created a federal deficit, only President Clinton has ever managed to deal effectively with this issue, and pass legislation that effectively circumvented a deficit accumulation.

President Clinton also signed another act that cut taxes and cut capital gains tax for individuals, as well as providing a child tax credit, and education incentives. President Bush has signed tax cuts into law every year, and affected the tax cuts that offered incentives to businesses, that had the intended effect of pulling us out of a mild recession, and encouraging businesses to create new jobs, to replace many of the manufacturing jobs lost to Mexico and China.

So, that by now, we're all quite used to having the tax visit each year, and either take or distribute taxes. We've all become accustomed to the stronghold that the IRS has on our weekly wages, our earned income, and the accountability we're forced to give, but there was a time when we were truly free of encumbrances, when money earned was money kept.

Student Loan Interest

As a parent or student, the need to be informed about the benefits of student loans, the extremely low interest rates, and the tax benefit they provide has increased tremendously over the last few years as education costs have risen, and the need for every deduction and credit has also increased. The Internal Revenue Service and the US government have now included student loan interest as a tax deductible item on the personal tax return. The second, and perhaps most important reason, is due to the fact that interest rates on student loans are beginning to climb, several percentage points.

As of August 1, 2005, the previous cap on the maximum student loan interest rate was repealed, and the new rates went into effect; what is the effect on existing student loans? What will the effect be on new student loans? How does this affect the bottom line of the students or parents tax return? These are questions that parents and students alike are seeking the answers to, prior to the rate change. Many of the organizations that offer student loan consolidation programs urged students to consolidate existing loans in order to lock in the low interest rate, while still available, as the new rates would definitely impact tax returns as the student begins to repay the loan, or the parent repays the loan.

Interest rates on federally subsidized loans do not have the tremendous impact on a student's finances when compared to unsubsidized or private issue loans. Deferred payment loans that also defer interest payments can generate extremely large additional amounts of debt for a student borrower because the loan is accruing interest on interest charges. Now, can you see how a change in interest rates would have a huge affect on student loans and student taxes?

In order to promote the advancement of continued education, the government has, over the last several years allowed the interest paid on student loans be a deduction on your tax return. This has helped ease some of the expense of college, but it isn't a direct form of relief. The individual claiming the deduction simply gets a portion of the interest deducted on their itemized schedule of deductions; it's not a dollar for dollar credit.

Deferred payment loans originally existed to create a buffer for the student borrower trying to attend school and work enough to keep up daily needs. Deferred payment allows the students to borrow, attend school without the worry of monthly loan payments, and then assume the responsibility for monthly payments upon completion of their degree. The government offers deferred payment loans to students in two forms, subsidized and unsubsidized. The subsidized loans are for students with a demonstrated financial need; the government pays the interest accrued until the student has finished or left school. Unsubsidized loans are not need based; the student is responsible for interest as it accrues on the loan. Either way, the interest is taken care of and paid monthly.

There are lenders today, who offer deferred payment loans simply because of the income they generate for the institution extending the loan. Students, who do not pay interest as it accrues, will pay interest charged on their interest balance each month. Many reputable lenders see this as an exploitation of the student, and do not even offer such a product.

Private loan products offered through lending institutions, where there are no federal lending requirements associated with this particular loan product and the student's school status in relation to financial need, have made a business of deferred payment loans. These very profitable loan products are often offered to students, who do not realize or necessarily understand the concept of the interest charge incurred on interest accrued.

Deferred payment loan products offered within the boundaries of the federally subsidized or unsubsidized guidelines are tremendously helpful to students and parents during these lean years of college funding; some of the private loan products, however, merely take advantage of the financial needs of student borrowers. Read carefully the terms and conditions of your loan and if offered the opportunity, make interest payments as the interest accrues. Your student loan debt at the end of the deferment period will be much smaller if the interest due each month has not been added to the amount due each month. In this way, you are only making interest payments, which are easily affordable, and you get to deduct the interest each year from your tax return.

A Tax and Government: By the People, For the People, Still?

Thomas Jefferson was quoted as saying that the government that governs least, governs best. Today, however, we seem to be headed in a completely different direction. We seem to think that the bigger the government the better the benefit and so more of the responsibilities of growth for the economy have been placed on the shoulders of our government. Was this a conscious decision by the American public, or was this a subversive action on the part of our government?

During the 1960s, when Franklin Roosevelt and the Congress of the United States implemented the "new deal" and unsuspecting citizenry welcomed this as a major step forward in the progress of the economic development of United States; many citizens saw this as a way to improve the standard of living for every individual. The "new deal" has in many ways were to accomplish its intended purpose, there are other areas, however, we are just the opposite has occurred. Today, more than ever, we have a tremendous reliance on "government welfare" and the public assistance programs that aid many of the nation's poor. Instead, however off encouraging independence and productivity from our citizens, it has created a true dependence upon our government to provide life's necessities. Instead of fostering growth and independence, it has created a third-generation welfare problem.

It has also generated a much larger federal government. In order to fund all the programs implemented during the "new deal" era, the government has imposed greater and greater taxation of the American public. In that entertain, when income tax was reinstated and became a way of life, the average and taxpayer paid 1% in tax; today, the average taxpayer pays almost 10% in income tax. The government now receives over $2 trillion in income tax, each year, and each year we watch as our government deficit grows; it continues to grow, because government continues to spend more than it receives.

Not all government spending is centered on welfare programs or public assistance programs. Some of the excess spending on the part of our government does to fund foreign aid, the war in Iraq, and pet programs for many of our congressmen. However, we are reaching a point in our country when government spending and welfare programs exceed the working class' ability to keep up. This is proven by the problems we're now experiencing and anticipating with our Social Security system.

In addition to the massive spending on the part of our government in support of welfare programs, we have now legislated many of our free enterprise and private sector businesses to the point that it is impossible to truly generate economic growth from a small business perspective. The taxes levied on and paid by small businesses, in conjunction with the regulations imposed by government that create additional spending, have backed the small businessman into a corner.

Government spending now accounts for almost 58% of the entire economic income of this country; less than 100 years ago, it accounted for only 12% of the economic income. This massive growth in government spending as a means to support the countries income and economy means that the average taxpayer must work 5 1/2 months to support government and government spending. This is not why our forefathers created government; the smaller our government the more innovative and creative our private sector businesses can become.

In addition to the excess in spending, the more government grows, the more government controls. So that, in addition to excessive taxes, we have excessive control. This country was made great because of the tremendous opportunity she offered the many immigrants who came to her shores. Now, thanks to the new deal and the welfare programs we don't offer our immigrants and opportunity to work, we offer them a check. Private sector businesses can no longer find employees at the minimum wage level, because welfare is more profitable.

Once again, we must refer back to Thomas Jefferson's words, "the government that governs least governs best", and hope that eventually this philosophy will be realized.

Tax Auditing

This is a topic almost everyone you speak those words to, would like to avoid. No one wants to experience an audit first hand; however, tax audits do not have to be the "monsters" we've made them out to be. There are audits for personal returns, corporate returns, and small business returns. Until recently, an understaffed IRS found it difficult to conduct a large quantity of audits. But now, be warned, their staff have increased, and so too will the audits.

What should you do to prepare and maintain your records, should you be chosen for an audit? Here's a little advice from the Internal Revenue Service.

Well, to understand the "real world" proportion of audits that are conducted, consider this: the IRS conducting only .79% of small firms during 2004; so, even though efforts have been stepped up, the percentage is still going to be small. Some of the more obvious items on your return that will peak the curiosity of the Internal Revenue are travel and entertainment expenses, depreciation, tax credits, charitable expenses, shipping expenses, and sales and returns. As a general rule, these are some of the expenses that are normally recorded in erroneously, or with false figures.

There are "licensing and other fees", another area of concern for the IRS that will flag audit personnel's interest. The big one right now, seems to be the internet search fees, and other internet related items, that are difficult to document, except via credit card records, and usually these are personal credit card records. Make sure that any information that relates to such a charge is carefully kept and matched to the correct credit card statement.

Advertising costs is another area for scrutiny. It has ties to the internet, also. But advertising expenses are often just that, expensive; there is room for error in record-keeping with advertising and exactly what constitutes advertising.

There are also percentages that alert the Internal Revenue and generate an interest when the variance from the national average is vastly different. Make sure if you have areas where the expenses where somewhat out of the norm, you document the reasons, and log expenses in the right category.

There are guides available from the IRS that are published to help industries and small businesses assure themselves they're following IRS regulations and common trouble spots. Why does the IRS furnish these guides? Because it's much better for you to correctly complete your tax return, and pay the tax due without auditing, than it is to perform and audit to correctly assess any tax due. These guides are known as Audit Technique Guides and they're available from the IRS, free of charge. They provide you with your industry standards, the most common mistakes made by these industries in their record keeping and tax reporting. These guides were developed by the IRS in order to train audit specialists about particular segments of business, so that when an audit was conducted, the auditor was knowledgeable in that particular field. So far, the training has proved invaluable, and the program is working, to the benefit of the business owners and the IRS, alike.

As with any segment of business, individual return, or corporate operation, your best defense is a good offense. If you've taken the time to keep adequate records, maintained good accounting practices with your records, and sought the services of a qualified tax specialist, you have nothing to worry about. The IRS doesn't really deserve the "bad" image they've been given. Their job is just like that of any other regulatory agency; they have laws and policies that must be enforced, they are the entity responsible for enforcing them. The people to be feared are the policy makers in Washington that are slowly regulating businesses and individuals into over taxation. Today, corporate America pays fewer taxes than ever before. Post WWII figures, indicated a close balance between individual tax liability and corporate tax liability, today the percentages are closer to 4 to 1 (80% of the tax is paid by individuals and small businesses). The really dangerous organization would be the body of government that is deciding the regulations, not the organization enforcing them.

Tax Evasion

What is tax evasion, and how does our government control it? That's a really big question to answer, so let's break it apart and answer it in two different paragraphs. Tax evasion is the intentional avoidance of tax due by a taxpayer, corporation, or other legal entity. There is a vast difference between the opportunity to minimize your tax liability and the direct avoidance of any responsibility. The tax laws and regulations of the Internal Revenue Service are there for the benefit of the taxpayer. If there is a way to reduce or minimize the amount of tax due, legally, by all means citizens are encouraged to take the break. There are all sorts of ways to commit tax evasion, and many famous cases have been tried, such as Al Capone and Willy Nelson.

When, as a taxpayer, you seek whatever legal means possible to avoid tax liability, you are guilty of no crime. It is your given right to seek a means to minimize your liability, in order to keep more of your money. However, when companies, individuals, or any other legal entities attempt to avoid their legal responsibility, we as a country suffer. The government operates on tax dollars. Tax dollars that everyone who has been deemed liable must provide, and if not provided, penalizes everyone.

Tax evasion has been a part of society for as long as there have been societies. Even during Roman rule, there were tax collectors, and individuals who evaded their payment of taxes. This country was founded on the precept that England charged an unfair tax on tea (and other various assorted sundry) to the point that the colonists were unfairly taxed, without a voice in the government. The Internal Revenue Service is charged with overseeing the regulation and prosecution of any person or entity that avoids payment of taxes due, and can assess penalties for those who succeed.

What tools does the Internal Revenue Service (IRS) use to control tax evasion? There are actually several means by which the IRS can control tax evasion, once they discover the crime has been committed. How do they detect tax evasion? The IRS has some 2800 special agents that are trained to gather information that is used to detect tax evasion; they have unlimited access to tax returns, the power to issue summons regarding needed financial information, and the right to seize or freeze monies in the attempt to collect the necessary financial information.

Once the tax evasion has been detected, the Internal Revenue Service can levy tax liens, seize assets, freeze money in checking and savings accounts, and garnish wages. Any and all properties held by the individual taxpayer can be seized, and sold at auction if no attempt is made to repay the liability. Everyone that is determined to be involved in an evasion of tax liability has the opportunity to be heard, to meet with the Internal Revenue Service, and receive a trial to determine if the accused party is guilty. It is generally in the individual's best interest to settle with the Internal Revenue Service if there is any possible doubt as to their innocence.

That's not to say that the Internal Revenue Service has always played fairly, or that they are free from mistakes. This is not so. There have been many instances of improper intelligence access, and errors on the part of the Internal Revenue. But, in the majority of cases, the tax evasion accusation was legitimate, and the individual charged was guilty. Many individual taxpayers rely on accountants and business managers to handle their financial affairs; in fact, many are not even aware of the status of their finances. It is however, ultimately, the individual taxpayer's responsibility to be held accountable for the information provided to the Internal Revenue Service. So, if you're going to be the one in front of the Internal Revenue, you should do yourself a favor and examine your return, understand what you're reading, and check the return for accuracy.

The History of the Internal Revenue Service

Do you ever wonder, how a country that revolted because of the unfair taxation of tea, came to be under the tight control of the Internal Revenue System? It seems kind of ironic, doesn't it, that the very reason we were founded, unfair taxation, is exactly where we are as a country today? How did we come up with our own office of taxation, and how long has it been in existence? This article examines how the Internal Revenue Service was formed, and how we arrived at our present day system.

The Internal Revenue Service was formed in 1862 when congress established the office of the Commissioner of Internal Revenue. This office was given the power over any form of taxation and the right to enforce those laws and regulations. Not much has changed since the income tax law of 1862, as far as the powers given to the Internal Revenue Service. The income taxation of the individual citizen has changed, somewhat drastically, however. The income tax was repealed in 1872, revived in 1894 and 1895 then laid to the side.

It wasn't until the 16th Amendment to the Constitution made the income tax a permanent part of the constitution, and a permanent fixture in 1913 and the growth of the Internal Revenue Service really began to thrive. The 16th Amendment gave Congress the authority to tax the income of both individuals and corporations that resulted in a tremendous increase in revenue. During the following 5 years, annual internal revenue collections passed the billion dollar mark rising to several billion dollars by 1920. Thanks to the next series of Wars, employment increased, and so did tax collections, rising even further into the billions of dollars. Withholding taxes were introduced in 1943, and this increased the number of individual taxpayers to well over 50 million; at the same time, tax collections increased by to $43 billion in 1945.

Every president since the term of Ronald Reagan has in some way, shape, form or fashion signed into law tax cuts that have affected the individual taxpayer, as well as the corporate tax payer. Almost every tax cut ever introduced, for some brief period of time created a federal deficit, only President Clinton has ever managed to deal effectively with this issue, and pass legislation that effectively circumvented a deficit accumulation.

President Clinton also signed another act that cut taxes and cut capital gains tax for individuals, as well as providing a child tax credit, and education incentives. President Bush has signed tax cuts into law every year, and affected the tax cuts that offered incentives to businesses, that had the intended effect of pulling us out of a mild recession, and encouraging businesses to create new jobs, to replace many of the manufacturing jobs lost to Mexico and China.

An overhaul of the Internal Revenue Service, and an attempt to upgrade their image in the eyes of the public, became a real concern for the IRS during the 90s, and it was also during this time, that the advent of the internet and the electronic filing options began to really take hold with the American public, and with the IRS. Today, electronic filing accounts for a large percentage of the income tax returns completed, and for many that will receive Earned Income Credit, it's an excellent opportunity to receive their refunds much faster.

Today, the IRS has been given a much more favorable rating by the American public, than in previous years, but it's thanks to a great effort on behalf of the employees and administrators of the IRS. Let's hope we continue to see a more cooperative relationship between the citizens of this country and the Internal Revenue Service.

The Internal Revenue Service

Do you ever wonder, how a country that revolted because of the unfair taxation of tea, came to be under the tight control of the Internal Revenue System? It seems kind of ironic, doesn't it, that the very reason we were founded, unfair taxation, is exactly where we are as a country today? How did we come up with our own office of taxation, and how long has it been in existence? This article examines how the Internal Revenue Service was formed, and how we arrived at our present day system.

The Internal Revenue Service, not as we know it today, was formed in 1862 when congress established the office of the Commissioner. This office was given complete control of the tax process in the United States, and the right to enforce all tax laws. Not much has changed since the income tax law of 1862, as far as the powers given to the Internal Revenue Service. The income taxation of the individual citizen has changed, somewhat drastically, however. The income tax was repealed in 1872, revived in 1894 and 1895 then laid to the side.

It wasn't until the 16th Amendment to the Constitution made the income tax a permanent part of the constitution, and a permanent fixture in 1913 and the growth of the Internal Revenue Service really began to thrive. The 16th Amendment gave Congress the authority to tax the income of both individuals and corporations that resulted in a tremendous increase in revenue. During the following 5 years, annual internal revenue collections passed the billion dollar mark rising to several billion dollars by 1920. Thanks to the next series of Wars, employment increased, and so did tax collections, rising even further into the billions of dollars. Withholding taxes were introduced in 1943, and this increased the number of individual taxpayers to well over 50 million; at the same time, tax collections increased by to $43 billion in 1945.

Every president since the term of Ronald Reagan has in some way, shape, form or fashion signed into law tax cuts that have affected the individual taxpayer, as well as the corporate tax payer. Almost every tax cut ever introduced, for some brief period of time created a federal deficit, only President Clinton has ever managed to deal effectively with this issue, and pass legislation that effectively circumvented a deficit accumulation.

President Clinton also signed another act that cut taxes and cut capital gains tax for individuals, as well as providing a child tax credit, and education incentives. President Bush has signed tax cuts into law every year, and affected the tax cuts that offered incentives to businesses, that had the intended effect of pulling us out of a mild recession, and encouraging businesses to create new jobs, to replace many of the manufacturing jobs lost to Mexico and China.

An overhaul of the Internal Revenue Service, and an attempt to upgrade their image in the eyes of the public, became a real concern for the IRS during the 90s, and it was also during this time, that the advent of the internet and the electronic filing options began to really take hold with the American public, and with the IRS. Today, electronic filing accounts for a large percentage of the income tax returns completed, and for many that will receive Earned Income Credit, it's an excellent opportunity to receive their refunds much faster.

Today, the IRS has been given a much more favorable rating by the American public, than in previous years, but it's thanks to a great effort on behalf of the employees and administrators of the IRS. Let's hope we continue to see a more cooperative relationship between the citizens of this country and the Internal Revenue Service.

You're Tax Dollars at Work

In case we should ever stop to question the government and the tax dollars of the US citizens has on the economy, let's take a look at the influence the government exerts over our daily lives, and the impact both good and bad of that influence.

The numbers are really staggering; the government controls, through direct spending about 43-45% of the economy. That's a truly amazing figure. Today more than ever, government spending accounts for almost as much of the economy as the private sector spending. During the late 30s and early 40s, right after the passage of the New Deal legislation, private sector controlled almost 90% of the economy. This should give you some idea as the drastic change we've experienced in only two generations. If you convert these percentages to real dollars and cents, this equates to roughly $13,000 in support by the individual citizen spent towards the government's taxation needs. When you turn this into working days, it equals 5.3 months of your work year are devoted to support government spending.

To step back, and clarify these statistics, first you must understand that the economy is divided basically into two sectors: there is one that is dependent upon federal, state, and local government spending, and this is known as the government sector, and then there's all others, known as the private sector. The government sector is funded by tax dollars collected from the individuals and businesses in this country. Therefore, whatever the government decides to spend and influence the economy with is basically funded by our tax dollars.

Total government spending controls $5.4 trillion dollars of the total spending, when you add the $1.4 trillion government imposed regulatory compliance spending the government actually controls almost 58% of the economy's national income. The disturbing factor for everyone involved here, is that this is a 3.5 times increase from a hundred years ago. That wouldn't be so disturbing if the rest of the economy had grown at the same rate, but it hasn't. It has seen a decline. The ability of private sector growth to produce living standard growth has been diminished over time, thanks to the fact that the government control has outgrown and overtaken the private sector control.

I don't think that's what our founding fathers had in mind when they wrote the Declaration of Independence, and declared their independence from the heavily governed England. They wanted less government control; The New Deal programs of the 30s, helped push us to a more "socialized" program of governing. One in which we look out for the masses, rather than relying on the initiative of human nature and private enterprise to take hold and provide individuals with the opportunities they need to better their lives.

Another interesting figure is the rate of growth for government employment compared with the growth of the population as a whole. While population has increased at a rate of 108%, government employment has increased by 476%; that's almost a 4 to 1 ratio in increase.

One of the biggest contributors to the increased government control comes from the special interest groups, and the ability of big business to lobby congress for programs, and changes in tax structure that benefits only a certain sector of the population. Another culprit is of course the socialized status of our government and the people it has tried to help. Government funded welfare and public assistance programs are a major contributor to the government spending programs.

This isn't what our forefathers intended, of that I'm quite certain. How do we attempt to correct this problem? No one is ready to answer this question, but here's an interesting statistic for you, if we don't soon correct the massive government spending, our children will pay $25,000 each year to support an overburdened and overbearing government.

Medical Expenses and Your Itemized Deductions

Thanks to the complexity of the United States tax codes, the system itself, and the variations of tax codes from state to state, completing your personal tax return and maximizing your deductions and exemptions to their fullest potential, is like trying to complete a mind-twisting maze. The average individual required to file a personal tax return has no grasp of the US tax system, and must therefore rely on one of the many tax professionals to complete their return. Quite often, deductions and exemptions are overlooked simply because of a lack of communication. The following article will discuss the medical deductions available to the individual tax payer, and the fact that qualifying for these deductions must be communicated to the tax preparer.

The medical deduction allowable on your personal federal income tax return is 7.5% of your adjusted gross income. The expenses you're allowed to deduct include medical, dental and eye care expense for anyone who qualifies as a dependent for your return. If you are self-employed, the premium deductions you can take at a rate of 100%, and if it happens to be a better benefit, and if you're self-employed, take the insurance premium deduction under your Schedule C deduction.

Who qualifies as your dependent, and what medical expenses incurred by that individual are deductible? Let's take a moment to clarify. A person will generally qualify as your dependent if they lived in your home for the entire year, you provided over half their support, and they meet the relationship test. And, oh yes, they must be a U.S. Citizen. What medical expenses are deductible? I think an easier question might be what is not deductible? You can't deduct expenses for which you are reimbursed, you can't deduct cosmetic surgery for which there is no valid medical reason for the procedure, and you can't deduct nonprescription medicine. That approach makes the list much smaller.

What information should you provide to your tax preparer? Information such as medical expenses you paid for yourself or your children the past year, any medical insurance premiums you may have paid; dental work, eye exams, laboratory expenses, overnight expense to travel for medical treatment and hearing exams to name the most common. Now I'm going to list a few things you might not have though about.

If you have trouble with your vision, and you require a Seeing Eye dog, the expense for the purchase and upkeep of the animal is a medical expense deduction. Your transportation expense to and from the doctor is deductible. Legal fees you incur in obtaining the necessary authority to treat someone for mental illness is a medical deduction. The use of artificial implants, such as teeth and limbs are deductible. Ambulance service is you're charged is a medical expense. Even having the lead paint removed from your home is a deductible medical expense, since many children are at risk for lead poisoning. There are some of the nontraditional treatment therapies available as medical deductions, acupuncture and Christian Science Practitioner fees are two of the more common, however, you should check with your service provider. Quite often, they will know if their services qualify as deductible.

As you can see, there are many items that are considered medically deductible that would not readily seem to be classified as a medical expense. There as also ways to maximize the items that are normally included in medical deductions, in order to get the most bang for your buck.

If you're receiving medical care that will be extended over the end of one tax year, and into the beginning of the next tax year, schedule as much of the expense during the last couple of months of the current tax year, that way you stand a better chance of including more of those dollars that are above the 7.5% mark of your adjusted gross income. If you are self-employed and must provide your family with health insurance, insure them as a part of your business; generally all members of the family will participate in a family business, therefore, you can enroll them as employees of the business and this makes the entire premium deductible.

Mortgage Interest and Your Itemized Deductions

For the average consumer who has managed to acquire credit card debt, automobile loans, and various other small debts, is the mortgage interest, especially with an interest only loan an answer to mortgage interest deductions and elimination of non-deductible interest?

What options does the average consumer have in accommodating the tax need in relation to the housing need? What about the interest only loan option on a new mortgage? Today's housing and mortgage market has seen a tremendous growth in mortgage packages, variety and amount. The mortgage interest deductible on the interest only loan option, once thought to have gone the way of the Edsel automobile, is back today and in use by the masses. The mortgage market has seen an unbelievable increase in the interest only loans from just a mere sliver of the market a few years ago, to around 25% of the market share today. That's huge growth, especially when you talk less than 5 years to experience that growth.

What benefit does the mortgage interest (especially the interest only loan) bring to the table, and does this benefit the homeowner as a taxpayer? This is one question the mortgage lender probably won't be able to answer for you, and one you probably won't think to ask. But you should, because it's one question that can make a difference to you and to your tax return and the amount of the mortgage interest that will actually provide you with a tax deduction.

Quite often, if your income is not exceedingly high, the interest on your mortgage and the amount you can deduct are one and the same. Even when you purchase a standard mortgage, your deduction percentile doesn't change; only the amount computed and that generally is within $100 dollars, whether it is an interest only or a standard mortgage. The only other great benefit to an interest only loan and tax breaks would be if you put the money in a 401(k), MSA, or IRA, and that would be another paper altogether.

The mortgage interest and especially the interest only loan is sold to the consumer as a way to afford more house, pay off credit card debt, or provide a means to fund a savings of some kind, and that's true, it can be used for that purpose.   And if you're considering paying off those high interest credit cards, the mortgage interest you're charged on the interest only loan is fully deductible, while the credit cards are not; a word of caution, however, make sure you eliminate the credit cards when you eliminate the credit card debt, otherwise you might find yourself right back where you began, just with less home equity.

Why has the market experienced such growth? It's not totally related to the tax benefit; the home mortgages of today satisfy a common desire for the consumer: instant gratification of bigger and better. Such is the case when it's time to make those needed repairs, or house expansion. A second mortgage makes it possible to retain the same monthly mortgage payment, and still pull a lot of equity out of your home. This may sound like the ultimate solution, but is it really? It also adds to the amount of interest an individual can deduct at the end of the year; and if income levels are growing, the interest expense must grow in order to keep up. Now, this is a somewhat skewed way of looking at the benefit of a mortgage, but it figures right into the same scheme as the elimination of credit card debt and saving for 401(k) s as a valid reason to borrow money against your home.

The mortgage and the resulting interest are great tools, when used by the right people, in the right situation. For the average consumer and long-term homeowner, unless you think a better deduction on your tax return is worth the forfeiture of equity in your home, you'd better think twice before re-financing with a second mortgage that generates more interest, but less equity.

Non-Profits and Tax Liability

Many of the Unites States' non-profit and charitable organizations are exempt from property taxes, income taxes, and many other forms of personal property taxes. The original intent of these regulations was to allow the non-profits to operate without the worry of raising money to pay for tax expenditures. But as time has passed, and many of the non-profit agencies have grown into political, economic and social giants there has been an ever-increasing demand for accountability.

Many of these non-profits are property owning, big businesses. They generate massive amounts of revenue, but because of their non-profit status, they are exempt from the very tax system that serves to keep them alive. There are many forces at work to keep the non-profits tax exempt, even if the reasons aren't so charitable.

Big business has also entered the non-profit sector of society and economics, and now some of the very charities that were once heavily dependent upon the tax revenue generated, are refusing to share in the responsibility that should be due their communities.

Once upon a time, non-profits were the institutions that immediately come to mind when we think about charitable organizations: hospitals, universities, and other public, community service organizations. Most of these organizations operated on shoe-string budgets, and had very little in the way of assets. Today, the scenario has changed incredibly, and although still listed as non-profit, these organizations are generating lots of income. They are now property owners in larger cities, some of the most desired properties belong to non-profit organizations; their facilities are nicer than anything privately owned, and the services are not necessarily provided free.

Today, there are so many classifications of non-profits that is virtually impossible for the average citizen to truly understand a true non-profit organization, from the thinly veiled borderline non-profits. This adds to the confusion, and as the political power of the non-profit organizations has grown, so too has the murkiness surrounding their tax liability. Thanks to the complexity of the situation, and the fact that federal regulations can differ dramatically from state, county, and city regulations, and these municipalities lack the funding to fight the complex situation, most of these organizations are never challenged as to their non-profit status, and no taxes are ever assessed.

Where does this leave our local economies? Often, out in the cold. The non-profit organizations within a city can be extremely numerous when you follow some of the complex guidelines that define "non-profit", and although the non-profit organizations are profiting handsomely from generated income, not necessarily revenue, the city, county, and state do not receive any funding or contribution from the organization.

As mentioned earlier, the political clout of these non-profit organizations has grown right along with their property assets, and you would be hard-pressed to succeed in changing some of the regulations and legalities that could affect the tax status of a non-profit. They have become what are known in Washington as "special interest groups" and their influence is far-reaching. From the religious groups, to the universities and research centers around America, they continue to gain handsomely without sharing in the tax burden. We have school systems that are starved for funding, but the counties and cities within which they operate, have no tax base to support them. We have school systems that also have leadership abuses that drain them of funding. As with their non-profit status, their leadership is questionable. The US tax system and the methods used for classification of organizations, businesses and other legal entities, needs an update urgently. Not only do businesses, profit and non-profit, shirk their tax liability; the government has made it extremely easy to accomplish that end.

Non-Profits and Tax Liability

Many of the Unites States' non-profit and charitable organizations are exempt from property taxes, income taxes, and many other forms of personal property taxes. The original intent of these regulations was to allow the non-profits to operate without the worry of raising money to pay for tax expenditures. But as time has passed, and many of the non-profit agencies have grown into political, economic and social giants there has been an ever-increasing demand for accountability.

Many of these non-profits are property owning, big businesses. They generate massive amounts of revenue, but because of their non-profit status, they are exempt from the very tax system that serves to keep them alive. There are many forces at work to keep the non-profits tax exempt, even if the reasons aren't so charitable.

Big business has also entered the non-profit sector of society and economics, and now some of the very charities that were once heavily dependent upon the tax revenue generated, are refusing to share in the responsibility that should be due their communities. Once upon a time, non-profits were the institutions that immediately come to mind when we think about charitable organizations: hospitals, universities, and other public, community service organizations. Most of these organizations operated on shoe-string budgets, and had very little in the way of assets. Today, the scenario has changed incredibly, and although still listed as non-profit, these organizations are generating lots of income. They are now property owners in larger cities, some of the most desired properties belong to non-profit organizations; their facilities are nicer than anything privately owned, and the services are not necessarily provided free.

Today, there are so many classifications of non-profits that is virtually impossible for the average citizen to truly understand a true non-profit organization, from the thinly veiled borderline non-profits. This adds to the confusion, and as the political power of the non-profit organizations has grown, so too has the murkiness surrounding their tax liability. Thanks to the complexity of the situation, and the fact that federal regulations can differ dramatically from state, county, and city regulations, and these municipalities lack the funding to fight the complex situation, most of these organizations are never challenged as to their non-profit status, and no taxes are ever assessed.

Where does this leave our local economies? Often, out in the cold. The non-profit organizations within a city can be extremely numerous when you follow some of the complex guidelines that define "non-profit", and although the non-profit organizations are profiting handsomely from generated income, not necessarily revenue, the city, county, and state do not receive any funding or contribution from the organization.

As mentioned earlier, the political clout of these non-profit organizations has grown right along with their property assets, and you would be hard-pressed to succeed in changing some of the regulations and legalities that could affect the tax status of a non-profit.

They have become what are known in Washington as "special interest groups" and their influence is far-reaching. From the religious groups, to the universities and research centers around America, they continue to gain handsomely without sharing in the tax burden. We have school systems that are starved for funding, but the counties and cities within which they operate, have no tax base to support them. We have school systems that also have leadership abuses that drain them of funding. As with their non-profit status, their leadership is questionable. The US tax system and the methods used for classification of organizations, businesses and other legal entities, needs an update urgently. Not only do businesses, profit and non-profit, shirk their tax liability; the government has made it extremely easy to accomplish that end.

State and Local Taxes

Small businesses owners are dependent upon each state for their liability when it comes to payroll taxes due a state because of the business operation.

Each state varies, and there are some states that do not withhold tax and require no state income tax filing; However if you operate a business within the United States, you will be required to withhold and deduct unemployment tax for each state in which you operate.

Generally, state tax rates on unemployment tax will vary slightly, depending upon the employment history of the business. Once in business long enough, a tax rate can be established based upon the employer's experience with benefit charges (employees who have drawn unemployment) and taxable payroll.

Taxes are deducted in the same manner as federal taxes, each pay period and filed with the applicable state on a monthly basis, just as federal depositors. Many accounting firms, however, recommend a weekly depositor account, so that the employer is not hit with extremely large taxes due. Most states will also require a quarterly information report comparable to the 941 federal forms and referenced in a like manner. Withholding rates on the state level are much lower than the federal rates and there are also limits of liability. As with Social Security, once a particular income level has been attained on the state level, the amount of the withholding may be reduced, and in some states is even eliminated.

Small businesses operating in one more than one state will be liable for payroll taxes in each state of operation. If you operate in multiple states, but do not maintain a permanent address, you should contact each state of operation to determine your liability and setup the necessary accounts for deductions. Quite often accountants that handle state taxes in your area will be aware of each state's filing requirements and be able to assist you in your filing requirement needs.

Your greatest concern on the state taxation level will be the unemployment tax that you are required to withhold. Your tax rating establishes the rate of your tax liability; new businesses are given a standard rating until an assessed rating can be determined based upon employee benefit charges and gross taxable payroll.

Local taxes are an even further extension of the employer withholding process, and businesses that operate in a particular state will generally be able to access information about a particular locality via their state's revenue office. Taxes withheld on the local level will not usually require a separate form, since local government entities will generally require that you file a copy of the state form with their local offices. They do not have the resources to develop separate forms and reporting procedures, and any monies due a local government municipality are forwarded from the state revenue department. Employers will file W-2 information and the information return accompanying W-2's with the IRS, the state agency, and then with any needed local municipality.   You don't withhold Medicare social security, or unemployment tax that the local level. Businesses are liable for withholding and reporting of the wages earned by each employee, and the timely filing of such withholding and reporting just with the federal and state agencies.

Local tax rates are substantially lower than those of the state level, and sometimes are referred to as a permit or license taxes. Some cities charge a flat rate comparable to a license is you don't live in the city where you work.

Small businesses can refer to individual state requirements via the Department of Revenue, Department of Industrial Relations, Employment offices, or Small Business Administration for direction and assistance in complying with all the necessary state and local laws. If any additional information is needed, it may be obtained thru the IRS website at www.irs.gov . There are numerous publications that provide direction and instructions for small businesses; among them are IRS Publication 15, Circular E

Employers Tax Guide, and links to individual state and local websites.

Tax Fraud

What is tax fraud, and how does our government control it? That's a really big question to answer, so let's break it apart and answer it in two different paragraphs. Tax fraud is the intentional avoidance of tax due by a taxpayer, corporation, or other legal entity. There is a vast difference between the opportunity to minimize your tax liability and the direct avoidance of any responsibility. The tax laws and regulations of the Internal Revenue Service are there for the benefit of the taxpayer. If there is a way to reduce or minimize the amount of tax due, legally, by all means citizens are encouraged to take the break. There are all sorts of ways to commit tax fraud, and many famous cases have been tried, such as Al Capone and Willy Nelson.

When, as a taxpayer, you seek whatever legal means possible to avoid tax liability, you are guilty of no crime. It is your given right to seek a means to minimize your liability, in order to keep more of your money. However, when companies, individuals, or any other legal entities attempt to avoid their legal responsibility, we as a country suffer. The government operates on tax dollars. Tax dollars that everyone who has been deemed liable must provide, and if not provided, penalizes everyone.

Tax fraud has been a part of society for as long as there have been societies. Even during Roman rule, there were tax collectors, and individuals who evaded their payment of taxes. This country was founded on the precept that England charged an unfair tax on tea (and other various assorted sundry) to the point that the colonists were unfairly taxed, without a voice in the government. The Internal Revenue Service is charged with overseeing the regulation and prosecution of any person or entity that avoids payment of taxes due, and can assess penalties for those who succeed.

What tools does the Internal Revenue Service (IRS) use to control tax fraud? There are actually several means by which the IRS can control tax fraud, once they discover the crime has been committed. How do they detect tax fraud? The IRS has some 2800 special agents that are trained to gather information that is used to detect tax fraud; they have unlimited access to tax returns, the power to issue summons regarding needed financial information, and the right to seize or freeze monies in the attempt to collect the necessary financial information.

Once the tax fraud has been detected, the Internal Revenue Service can levy tax liens, seize assets, freeze money in checking and savings accounts, and garnish wages. Any and all properties held by the individual taxpayer can be seized, and sold at auction if no attempt is made to repay the liability. Everyone that is determined to be involved in an evasive or fraudulent act of tax liability has the opportunity to be heard, to meet with the Internal Revenue Service, and receive a trial to determine if the accused party is guilty. It is generally in the individual's best interest to settle with the Internal Revenue Service if there is any possible doubt as to their innocence.

That's not to say that the Internal Revenue Service has always played fairly, or that they are free from mistakes. This is not so. There have been many instances of improper intelligence access, and errors on the part of the Internal Revenue. But, in the majority of cases, the tax fraud accusation was legitimate, and the individual charged was guilty. Many individual taxpayers rely on accountants and business managers to handle their financial affairs; in fact, many are not even aware of the status of their finances. It is however, ultimately, the individual taxpayer's responsibility to be held accountable for the information provided to the Internal Revenue Service. So, if you're going to be the one in front of the Internal Revenue, you should do yourself a favor and examine your return, understand what you're reading, and check the return for accuracy.

The History of the Social Security System

In the years before the Great Depression, not very much thought had been given to the economic well-being of the country's elderly, nor about the economic health of the country as a whole. But the Great Depression changed all that, and it changed the way government looked at the population of this great nation. On August 14, 1935 the Social Security Act was passed into law, and this country would be forever changed.

What did the Social Security Act mean for the average American when the bill passed? It was the age of the "New Deal" and Franklin Roosevelt was determined to leave this country in better shape than when he arrived. And he did. Today, Social Security if often touted by the Social Security Administration as the most successful domestic government program, and it is. But it is also one teetering on the brink of trouble; massive trouble.

Today, Social Security is on the border of reaching a level of adequate funding; in fact, if you plan to collect security benefits after the year 2017, the problem may turn out to be a serious one. Why are we experiencing the shortfall? There are actually several contributors to the problem, and none of them can be identified as the primary contributor. A declining birthrate, and increased lifespan, and an ever widening gap between the poorer wage earners of the nation and the higher wage earners have left the administration for the funding problem.

In fact, according to projections made by the trustees of the Social Security Administration, the fund will actually begin spending more than it takes in around the year 2015 to 2017, and past those years, the amount collected will only pay about two thirds of the benefits guaranteed to retirees, survivors, and the disabled. Not a pretty picture for those of us born after 1959, uh?

Is the problem really as bad as we are led to believe? It all depends on whose side you are listening to. Proponents of the privatization of Social Security say the problem is tremendous; still others contend that with the current growth of the US economy, there's really no need for the proposition of privatization of Social Security funding. In fact, the Bureau of Labor Statistics is expected announce adjustments to the Consumer Price Index that is used to calculate, Social Securities annual cost-of-living adjustment, or COLA. The result of this change is that early next year the Social Security Trustees are supposed to report that Social Security's long-term actuarial deficit is less than it was just one year ago. Where does this leave the advocates of privatization? Not in a very good position.

There will be, and must be, concessions on made on behalf of American citizens. The normal retirement age or NRA will surely be extended even further, possibly reaching into a retirees 70th birthday. The tax cap that is a traditional part of Social Security could be eliminated, just as it was with the Medicare tax cap in 1993. In fact, in light of the ever extending gap between low-wage earners and high wage earners, it would be one of the most common sense approaches to the increase needed in social security funding. In eliminating the social security tax cap, it is perhaps the easiest way, and the most easily factored way to remain solvent forever. If the tax cap were to be lifted, we would never have to worry about funding social security. You really don't hear too much about this option, because many of your wealthier individuals don't really want to pay social security past the point that is now required.

Advocates of the lift argue that if the lower wage earning Americans must pay tax all year, higher wage earners should also be required to contribute on a continual basis. After all, they're going to be eligible for higher monthly premiums, why shouldn't they be required to continue in efforts to help fund the program?

The Widening Income Gap: Rich vs. Poor

You would think that as a nation we suffer equally in economic downturns, but recent Census Bureau data, indicates otherwise. I know that you, as well as I, have always heard, the rich get richer, and the poor get poorer. But no one actually believed that until these recent findings proved the theory true.

Once upon a time in this country, there wasn't a great distinction between the higher-income, the middle-income and the lower-income. Maybe there was greater distinction between the truly wealthy and the well-to-do, but that was the greatest gap. That's not the picture we look at today.

The losers, here, and I state loser with the plural emphasis, have been the middle and low-income Americans. Although there have been economic gains in this country, the gains have been on the part of the higher-end wage earners, not the bread and butter wage earners that helped to build America. The corporate executives, the presidents, the positions that are commission, bonus, and incentive dependent have seen the growth. The middle and lower income Americans have seen only shortfalls.

On the average, 45 out of 50 states have witnessed increasing income gaps over the last 20 years, and that is a frightening statistic. What does this say about our economy, the regulations under which we all live, and the attitudes of our lawmakers (who by the way, are among the higher-end wage earners)? It certainly seems a long way from the principles upon which this country was founded, and grew in the early years. The principles we believed and operated under then, were that hard work should pay off. That for any individual willing to come to America and work hard, there was a life of prosperity, not poverty. Today, we are living a realization that this is merely an ideal, not a philosophy of our government and lawmakers.

We have had the strongest economy ever over the last twenty to thirty years, and the fact that even under these excellent conditions, we have failed to close a gap spells serious problems; that we witnessed its further widening is an affront to the hard working, honest citizens of this country. What does this say to our approaching generation of workers? That fat corporate bonuses, the Enron and HealthSouth scandals, and the day of "corporate dominance" is the successful path to follow. Pay no heed to the working man, the unskilled laborer, the production worker in a non-union plant.

What do the statistics revealed in the census say to us? Here are just a few: In some southern states, the poorest family's incomes increased by less than $1000, the richest family's incomes increased by an average of $40,000. (This doesn't include bonuses and incentive pay). The ratio of bottom and top income measurements revealed that for many of the 45 states, there is a 10 to 1 difference; in other words, the top income measurements were 10 times those of the bottom income measurements. To give you a point of reference, during the 1970s, there was not one single state where the difference was greater than 3. Amazing information, is it not?

What are the contributing factors in this completely evident see-saw relationship? Economic trends and government policy are the largest contributors, and both can be used to turn this trend around. The question facing most of voting America today, is will we demand a turnaround? Reforming the tax system, from state to federal levels, examining our minimum wage laws, implementing educational programs that further encourage higher education, and demanding more accountability from corporate

America would go a long way towards correcting a terrible and growing problem. If all members of a society are contributing to the growth of that society, all members should share in the prosperity. That is a basic principle upon which a democracy operates; the harder you work, the greater your opportunity and prosperity. Currently, we're not headed in this direction. The rich are getting richer, and the poor are suffering.

What is a Dependent?

Other than fitting the description of a constant liability, what other qualifying attributes must one have, to be classed as a dependent, and how do you determine this for tax purposes? The following paragraphs explain the qualifying tests for determining dependency as it relates to your tax status, liability and available credits. First, we need to make you aware that there are two different types of dependents. There

There are several "qualifying tests" an individual must pass, in order to be qualified as a dependent on a US 1040 tax return. The tests for dependency are centered around the actual support tests that the candidate must pass; first, the qualifying individual must be the taxpayer's child, stepchild, foster child, sibling or stepsibling, or a descendent of one of these (such as a niece or nephew), second the qualifying individual must have the same principal residence as the taxpayer for more than half the year and there are exceptions for children of divorced parents, kidnapped children, and for children who were born or died during the year, third the qualifying individual must be under the age of 19, or 24 if a full-time student and fourth, the qualifying individual must not have provided for more than one-half of their own support during the year. There are some additional rules that a dependent must pass, that really have nothing to do with the amount of support provided, but do determine their eligibility as US citizens and the ability to be considered for dependency. First, the qualifying individual must be a US citizen or national, and their marital status must be single, unless the are married but did not file a joint return for that year, or there was no tax liability that existed for either spouse had they filed separately.

If the qualifying individual can pass all four of the above described qualifying tests, as well as the additional rules, then any of the deductions, exemptions, and credits that are available can be used. For instance, child care expenses, child tax credits, dependent care expenses, earned income credit, and any associated itemized deductions may be claimed if the qualifying individual is determined eligible.

Determining eligibility in many cases means the difference between owing tax on your return, and the eligibility to file as head of household, and receive a refund that would include earned income credit. The earned income tax credit is a negative tax, and an attempt by the government to provide lower and poverty level income families with the opportunity to receive much needed assistance with caring for and supporting their families. Today, however, the earned income credit is becoming an opportunity for some segments of the public to abuse the goodwill of their government and falsify claims of dependency qualifications.

The child and dependent care expenses cover things like daycare, after school care programs, and any other form of paid care that is necessary for the qualifying individual to receive while the taxpayer is away at work. The only thing to watch here is that all qualifying individuals for the child and dependent care expenses must be under the age of 13.

The child tax credit is comparable to the earned income credit, in that it is a straight credit, dollar for dollar deduction of your tax liability. The child tax credit may only be taken by individuals with a qualifying dependent that is under the age of 17.

As you undertake the task of determining if your dependent meets the qualifying tests, and can actually provide some benefit in tax reduction at the end of the year, remember that it may take a little work, but the potential payoff could be well worth the time it takes to determine if you are single with no dependents, or head of household with a dependent and the opportunity to claim earned income credit, child care expense deductions, as well as file for the child tax credit. The result could be amazing!

When Do You File a Tax Return?

Every year, millions of Americans get ready to pay up to Uncle Sam, or get ready to collect from Uncle

Sam; when did this become the great day that it is for taxpayers, and when are we actually required to file a tax return? Let's take a look at the beginnings of the tax date of April 15 and why it was chosen?

The first known income tax that Americans were legally required to pay was enacted during the 1860s, and the Presidency of Abraham Lincoln. The Civil War was proving very costly to fund, and the President and Congress created the Commissioner of Revenue and enacted a law requiring citizens to pay income tax.

Originally, the deadline for completing and filing your individual income tax was not April 15th. In the beginning, it was first set for March 1st. Then, during 1918, Congress pushed the date out to March 15th. Then, in the great overhaul of 1954, the date was once again moved forward to April 15th, and this is where it remains today. But, it has only been set this way for a little over 50 years. That's not very long, in historical terms, and it could possibly be changed again.

If you are an individual tax payer, you are required to file either a return or an extension of time to file (Form 4868) by April 15th. Corporate and other legal entities are required to file their tax return by March 15th, and if not, they also must file an extension of time to file. What this extension does not do, is to extend the amount of time you have to pay any taxes due the government. So, if you are unable to ready your personal or business financial information in a timely manner, and have no reasonable estimate as to the amount of tax you may owe, you can expect to pay some form of penalty.

In the years following WWII, the burden of tax responsibility was shared fairly equally by the corporate world and the individual tax payer. Today, however, the shift has been toward more responsibility on the part of the individual, and less on the business backs. To demonstrate how special interests have begun to overtake American politics, during 1867, public opinion was so strong, and the outcry of the general public so loud, that the President and Congress repealed the income tax law, and from 1868 until 1913 almost all of the revenue for government operation came from the sale of liquor, beer, wine, and tobacco.

An interesting time during the formation and eventual taxation of America occurred during 1918. Until that point in time, the vast majority of revenue for government funding came from alcoholic beverage sales. In 1919, Congress passed an amendment to the Constitution that made it illegal to manufacture or sell alcohol; what would replace the revenue? American income tax was the proposed solution, and we've been paying since. Although during the great years known as Prohibition, many "revenue agents" spent their days tracking down "moon shiners" not tax evaders, the American citizen, the individual taxpayer took on the heavy burden of supporting government revenue, and it has become heavier with each passing year.

Then, during 1942, the Revenue Act of 1942 was passed and the "New Deal" era was begun. Since that point in time, government control, power, and expenditures has continued to increase at a phenomenal rate, and today the American taxpayer supports a trillion dollar giant known as the United States government. This ravenous beast consumes more than 10% of our earned income each year, and if the Social Security Administration has their way, will continue to consumer even more of our weekly earnings. We can foresee no other relief in sight.

Currently, all the tax regulations for this country are the responsibility of the Internal Revenue Service, and there are four major divisions of this government office: the Wage and Investment, Small/Business Self-Employed, the Large and Midsize Business and the Tax Exempt and Government Entities. Each division has responsibilities as they pertain to their individual specialty.

You're Tax Status

How do you determine your tax status and what are the differences between each one? Although not a tough question, it can mean a lengthy answer, and I'm afraid in this situation, it's going to be a lengthy response.

There are five ways in which you can classify yourself for your tax filing status: single, married filing jointly, married filing separately, head of household or qualifying widower with dependent child. The remainder of this article will examine each of these, and how you determine your correct status. Please note here, that if more than status will apply to you, you should choose the status that provides for the greatest tax benefit.

Let's start with the simple one: single. Determining your status as a single filer should be a simple one, but you would be amazed at the different situations that exist that can qualify the taxpayer as single. For instance, if you are legally separated at the year end, then you are considered single for the entire year. If you have no dependents and you are unmarried, you are considered single. There are other conditions under which you are considered single, such as annulled marriages. If you obtain an annulment of your marriage, then you are considered single as though the marriage never existed, even if you filed joint returns in earlier years. If you obtain a divorce in one year, simply to be able to file separate returns as single individuals, but remarry during the next year, you are considered married, and should have filed returns as married filing jointly or separately, not single.

If you meet all the rules of the single tax status, but you have a dependent, or you are widowed during the year, and have dependents, your filing status would be head of household or widow(er) with qualifying dependent child, not single.

How do you determine your status as a married taxpayer? Well, there are simple qualification tests that determine your legal filing status and if you're considered as "married". If you are legally married and living together as husband and wife, you would of course be considered married. If you are living together in a common law marriage that is recognized in the state in which you reside, or the state where the common law marriage began, then you are considered to have a filing status of married. You are also considered to be married if you reside with another individual as husband and wife and you're not formally divorced or legally separated.

Now, there are certain extenuating circumstances that must be considered before deciding your legal filing status. For instance, if you were widowed during the year and do not remarry, you may file as married with your deceased spouse for the year in which he or she passed, and then file as a widow(er) with qualified dependents for the next two years, provided you do not remarry. If you remarry within the year that your spouse was deceased, you would file as married with your current spouse, and file your deceased spouse as married filing separately. It's truly amazing at the unique and odd situations that are created by we taxpayer's and even more unique in the ways that they affect our tax situation.

Returns

If you are married and choose to file a joint return, your tax status would be married filing jointly. All income to the household must be included on the one return, and both spouses must sign and date prior to submitting the return to the Internal Revenue. All exemptions, deductions, and credits are also reported on the joint return; in addition to sharing joint filing status, you also share joint responsibility and liability for the information reported on the tax return. You can however, ask for relief from joint responsibility, in the following three ways: innocent spouse relief, separation of liability for spouses who have not lived together for the previous 12 months, or equitable relief which essentially shares the liability between the filers.

There are sometimes reasons that a spouse cannot sign the tax return, one of the more interesting situations exists when the spouse is away in a combat zone for the military. In this type of situation, you may sign for your spouse, and attach a separate information statement that explains why it was necessary for you to sign.

As you can see, choosing a tax filing status, and then understanding your responsibilities and rights, can be a very tedious, and frustrating experience.

As you can see, these articles cover the majority of topics that are of interest to the average individual taxpayer, and are written in everyday format, that makes for not only interesting reading, but easy absorption. I hope you have found these articles to be of some assistance, and hopefully some use to your tax and financial status come April 15th!

Please remember, this ebook is for entertainment purposes only, and you should consult a professional for true expert advice on taxation in the United States.